"*Strength from Within* provides healthcare practitioners with an invaluable tool and resource to prepare for an unfortunate, unavoidable, and likely event during one's career in this field. Jeff Krompier, one of the most capable and seasoned attorneys in the defense medical malpractice arena, enlightens his audience with a thorough, comprehensive, and accurate portrayal of facing a professional malpractice lawsuit. I particularly found his detailed attention to components of The Trial to be of great value and importance. I would recommend this read to all healthcare providers, a fantastic guide to the beginner as well as those who have had the misfortune of being sued and are familiar with the litigation process."

Joseph LaVerghetta, Esq.
Claims Consultant, Northeast & NY
MedPro Group

"As a practicing physician, *Strength from Within* is a timely, pragmatic, and deeply reassuring guide to navigating one of the most emotionally and professionally challenging experiences a doctor can face: being named in a malpractice lawsuit. Written by seasoned defense attorney Jeffrey A. Krompier, the book demystifies the legal process with clarity and empathy, offering a step-by-step roadmap from the moment of service through trial. The author's tone is both authoritative and compassionate, reinforcing that a malpractice suit is not a measure of incompetence, but often an unfortunate byproduct of modern clinical practice. This book is a valuable resource for navigating the emotional and procedural challenges of litigation with confidence and composure."

Kumar G. Sinha, M.D.
Orthopaedic Surgeon

"Most physicians will practice their specialties for four or five decades and have hundreds of thousands of patient encounters. *Strength from Within* is a must read for what every medical practitioner needs to know when faced with a malpractice suit. Krompier, a Super Malpractice Lawyer, details what medical schools should teach on this important subject."

Margaret Ravits, M.D.
Dermatologist
Clinical Associate Professor
Columbia University
College of Physicians and Surgeons

"*Strength from Within* is extremely well-written and provides great insight and a roadmap for every practitioner facing the challenge and uncertainty of being confronted with a lawsuit. Mr. Krompier translates his extensive legal experience into practical working knowledge of the litigation process."

Debbie Lloyd, MBA, MSN, RN, CPHRM
Claims Consultant, Northeast & NY
MedPro Group

"*Strength from Within* is a concise, poignant and entertaining read for any would be medical malpractice defendant. Mr. Krompier uses his vast experience as an outstanding, pre-eminent trial lawyer to offer tips, guidance and support techniques to prepare a defendant for the long rigors of the litigation process. Following the advice and counsel contained in *Strength from Within* will provide the framework for the best possible outcome for any medical malpractice defendant."

James J. Gleason, Jr.
Claims Division Manager, Northeast
MedPro Group

"The anxiety which a physician senses when an adverse outcome occurs during clinical practice too often revolves around the concern of possibly being accused of medical malpractice. In *Strength from Within*, Jeff Krompier explores the issues involved in a malpractice claim, from allegations to resolutions, in a clear, detailed manner. He describes the legal process to help anyone going through such an unfortunate process be able to handle all issues objectively. One is taken step by step through malpractice litigation enabling a physician to gain control of the process and achieve the best outcome. This book is a masterpiece which should be required reading for all physicians."

Stephen Winters, M.D.
Electrophysiologist

"Mr. Krompier has created a wonderfully and beautifully written guide to the confusing world of malpractice. Mr. Krompier is one of the nation's premier malpractice defense attorneys. His book is a refreshing look at the complex world of current malpractice litigation. As a defendant, one would find this well written book particularly useful and I would highly encourage its reading. Someone going to trial in a malpractice case without reading this book and gaining its unique insights would do so at their own peril. As a physician, I personally am very glad to have the good fortune to have this book on my desk."

Eric Uhrik, D.O.
Neurologist

"*Strength from Within* is an indispensable guide for medical and nursing professionals navigating the increasingly litigious landscape of healthcare. Timely and comprehensive, this book serves as a vital resource for anyone facing a medical malpractice lawsuit, offering not just legal education but also crucial emotional support.

From the moment a practitioner is "served" with a complaint, the book meticulously outlines each stage of the litigation process. It demystifies complex legal terms like compensatory and punitive damages, provides clear instructions on alerting insurance carriers, and offers actionable advice for initial responses, such as critical importance of not altering patient records. The chapters on engaging with defense counsel, understanding basic discovery tools like interrogatories and depositions, and preparing a Curriculum Vitae are exceptionally practical, anticipating common anxieties and providing concrete steps.

What truly sets *Strength from Within* apart is its empathetic approach. It acknowledges the immense stress, doubt, and frustration that accompany a lawsuit, actively working to transform feelings of weakness into strength. By explaining the process from initial complaint through trial preparation and the trial itself, the author empowers healthcare providers to understand their role, manage expectations, and participate effectively in their defense. This book is a must-read for any medical professional, offering clarity, confidence, and a much-needed sense of control during a challenging time."

Hany Gaafer-Ahmed, M.D.
Obstetrician/Gynecologist

"Brilliantly written and easy to understand! Attorney Jeffrey Krompier has expertly crafted a must-have manual for medical professionals at EVERY level—whether it is the student of medicine first finding out that lawsuit involvement could be a very real possibility of their profession, or the seasoned medical professional—everyone in medicine will benefit from reading this book. Quick and easy-to-read, this is the legal blueprint every medical professional needs!"

Michelle Mora, D.O.
Neurologist

"As a medical malpractice defense attorney for forty years, I highly recommend Mr. Krompier's comprehensive and insightful book. If you, as a healthcare professional are named as a defendant in a medical malpractice case, this book will guide you through the trials and tribulations of the entire litigation process. Well done Mr. Krompier."

Joseph DiCroce, Esq.
DiCroce, McCann & Farman, LLC

"Mr. Krompier has gone above and beyond drafting the typical "how to" publication and has instead created a simplified, yet exquisitely detailed descriptor of the entire malpractice lawsuit journey those physicians whom are served must travel. He carefully balances a personally supportive narrative with detailed objective describing of the entire process using an easily read descriptive voice throughout this publication.

For any physician whom has had to face the circumstances surrounding a malpractice lawsuit, this publication's content not only serves as a comprehensive event outline descriptor of the process, in its entirety, but shares experiences Mr. Krompier has compiled to be able to recommend effective methods by which served physicians can best respond and psychologically cope with each step as the requisite legal processes unfold.

His shared viewpoint is one of empathy, factual information exchange, and shall serve as an effective guide to best assist any doctor whom may be served and face a presumptive practice negligence claim.

I commend Mr. Krompier for taking the time to create a supportive narrative of this depth and style, one that will easily serve as both an educational reference and step by step informational resource for any physician in practice today. Bravo, Mr. Krompier. Well done and thank you for this important literary contribution."

Jamie R. Wisser, M.D., FACS
Plastic Surgeon

"Mr. Krompier provides an in-depth, practical, and easy-to-understand description of what a defendant can expect to experience in a malpractice lawsuit. Drawing on his many years of experience as a malpractice defense attorney, he demonstrates a keen awareness of the ever-evolving landscape of malpractice litigation. Throughout the book, he offers invaluable insights and practical guidance that will thoroughly prepare any defendant for the road ahead. This is a must-read for healthcare clinicians, executives, risk managers, and legal counsel alike."

Keah Buck, RN, BSN, MJ, MBA, CPHRM
Director\Risk Management, Claims & Insurance
St. Joseph's Health

"Strength from Within is a clear and focused guide for healthcare professionals who find themselves facing the daunting and emotionally draining process of a medical malpractice lawsuit. It provides a straight forward roadmap of the litigation process from the initiation of the lawsuit through resolution via trial or settlement. Jeff Krompier brings his vast experience to bear in clarifying what is often a confusing and complicated legal system. His practical advice and recommendations are spot on. *Strength from Within* is an invaluable resource for any healthcare provider who wants to be prepared, emotionally and professionally, to navigate the storm of a malpractice claim. I will be recommending it to my own clients."

David C. Donohue, Esq.
Farkas & Donohue, LLC

"Jeff is well-versed in the medical malpractice arena. His background, experience, and knowledge shine in his book. I have the utmost confidence and trust in Jeff as defense counsel on behalf of my insureds."

Jamie Vamvakas, JD, RPLU
*Second Vice President, Claim
Executive | Claims Division
GenStar Insurance Services, LLC
Member of the Berkshire Hathaway
Family of Companies*

"I have known Mr. Krompier for many years and am certain that if you need his services, you will be in great hands. It is admirable that he has taken the time to share his knowledge and expertise with people who need them. Doctors are never taught and are not prepared for the unfortunate reality of medical malpractice claims. This book gives you a quick and realistic view of what to expect. Thank you Jeff!!"

Idrees Ahmad, M.D.
Anesthesiologist

"For health care professionals, few experiences are as professionally and personally devastating as facing a malpractice lawsuit. In *Strength from Within*, defense attorney Jeffrey A. Krompier, Esq. transforms what could be a paralyzing ordeal into a manageable journey with his expertly crafted roadmap through medical litigation.

Drawing from his decades in the courtroom, Mr. Krompier delivers more than just legal advice— he provides a comprehensive survival guide that addresses every aspect of the malpractice experience. From the moment a physician or nurse receives that dreaded summons through the final gavel, this book offers clear, actionable strategies for navigating each phase of litigation. Mr. Krompier's practical insights cover everything from deposition tactics to courtroom presence, ensuring readers can actively participate in their defense rather than simply endure it.

What truly distinguishes this book is its dual focus on both legal strategy and emotional resilience. Mr. Krompier understands that malpractice suits attack not just professional reputations but personal well-being. His compassionate approach addresses the psychological challenges defendants face while providing concrete tools for collaboration with defense counsel, meticulous documentation, and strategic testimony preparation.

Whether you're facing your first lawsuit or have experienced multiple claims, *Strength from Within* offers invaluable guidance that transforms a potentially career-defining crisis into an opportunity for growth and renewed confidence. This isn't merely a legal reference—it's an essential resource that every health care provider should have within his/her personal library."

Sheldon H. Deluty, M.D.
Anesthesiologist

"*Strength from Within* is a truly well-written and exceptionally valuable resource, making it a must-read for anyone involved in a medical malpractice lawsuit. The book clearly outlines the intricacies of a malpractice claim process and offers crucial guidance on the "dos and don'ts." Beyond the legal specifics, it also serves as an excellent guide for maintaining composure and navigating what can be a very trying process. I found the content to be incredibly clear and practical."

Ajay Goyal, M.D., FACS
General & Bariatric Surgeon

"*Strength from Within: A Guide to Success as a Medical Malpractice Defendant* is an excellent resource for the health professional with or without a pending court case. Mr. Krompier takes the reader step by step through the complex legal process yet is easy to read and understand. This publication answers "what's next?" while clarifying the roles of the malpractice defense attorney and defendant. In the litigious environment in which we live, this reference should be a staple on your bookshelf."

Robert Levine, M.D.
Anesthesiologist

"Jeff Krompier has appeared many times before me and tried a medical malpractice case to verdict, by a jury. He secured a complete defense verdict. Jeff is always well prepared and is relentless in his representation of his client. He is a consummate trial lawyer, who has repeatedly earned my respect and admiration. His well-written book captures the essence of a medical malpractice case and is an essential tool to help medical professionals successfully navigate through the process."

Hon. Raymond A. Reddin
Superior Court Judge of New Jersey (ret.)

Strength from Within

Now that COVID-19 is behind us and the unprecedented public support for healthcare providers has waned, it is anticipated that physicians and nurses will again become malpractice defendants to a remarkable degree. In fact, the post-COVID-19 surge in lawsuits against medical and nursing professionals is likely to continue for the foreseeable future.

Presented here is a comprehensive review of what a newly named defendant can expect as well as how best to assist in the matter's defense from inception through trial. This book will provide an education about the litigation process and help the defendant succeed under difficult circumstances. Ultimately, it will serve as a source of strength when feelings of weakness, doubt, frustration, and anger surface.

Strength from Within

A Guide to Success as a Medical Malpractice Defendant

Jeffrey A. Krompier, Esq.

Routledge
Taylor & Francis Group

A PRODUCTIVITY PRESS BOOK

Designed cover image: Shutterstock

First published 2026
by Routledge
605 Third Avenue, New York, NY 10158

and by Routledge
4 Park Square, Milton Park, Abingdon, Oxon, OX14 4RN

Routledge is an imprint of the Taylor & Francis Group, an informa business

ISBN: 978-1-032-60412-1 (hbk)
ISBN: 978-1-032-60411-4 (pbk)
ISBN: 978-1-003-45900-2 (ebk)

DOI: 10.4324/9781003459002

Typeset in Garamond
by Deanta Global Publishing Services, Chennai, India

To my wife Angela for her love and support

Contents

Preface

So, it's been an uneventful day in your office up to this point and then…it happens. A nondescript individual appears in your waiting room with papers in hand. What you see is a Summons and Complaint naming you as a defendant in a medical malpractice lawsuit. You retreat to your office, sit at your desk, and with trepidation, slowly read the first page of the Complaint. You see the name of the plaintiff, a name you recognize, and your eyes widen as you try to comprehend the claims in the Complaint. You find yourself shaking your head in disbelief, certain that you never acted improperly at any time, despite claims to the contrary. You place the Complaint on your desk, lean back in your chair and uncomfortably think about what lies ahead.

About the Author

Jeffrey A. Krompier, Esq., is the founder and managing partner of the Parsippany, NJ, law firm which bears the name Krompier Law Group LLC. He is admitted to the bars of New Jersey and New York. Mr. Krompier is a 1977 magna cum laude and college honors graduate of Rutgers University and received both Phi Beta Kappa and Rutgers Scholar designations. In 1980, Mr. Krompier graduated from Seton Hall University School of Law, where he was an Associate Articles Editor of the Law Review and a judicial intern to the late Honorable Lawrence Whipple of the US District Court for the District of New Jersey. Upon graduation, Mr. Krompier served as judicial law clerk to the late Honorable Bertram Polow of the New Jersey Superior Court, Appellate Division, and thereafter began the private practice of law. In 1982, Mr. Krompier joined a medical malpractice defense firm where he practiced until 1986, when he founded his current firm, which is devoted to defending healthcare professionals in malpractice matters.

In 1988, the New Jersey Supreme Court certified Mr. Krompier as a Civil Trial Attorney. Throughout his career, Mr. Krompier has been recertified six times (1995, 2002, 2007, 2012, 2017, and 2022) by the New Jersey Supreme Court as a Civil Trial Attorney. In 2012, he received certification in Civil Trial Advocacy by the ABA-accredited National Board of Trial

Advocacy and certification in Civil Pretrial Practice Advocacy by the ABA-accredited National Board of Civil Pretrial Practice Advocacy. In 2017 and 2022, Mr. Krompier was recertified in both Civil Trial Law and Civil Practice Advocacy by the National Board of Trial Advocacy. He is a member of the American Bar Association, the American Board of Trial Advocates with Advocate ranking, and is a lifetime charter member of Rue Ratings' Best Attorneys of America.

For the last 19 consecutive years (2007–2025), he was named a New Jersey Super Lawyer and has been listed in *Super Lawyers* magazine, corporate counsel (2009–2011) and business (2011–2018) editions. In 2014, Mr. Krompier was named an Elite American Lawyer and honored for excellence in the law (2014–2015) by Worldwide Registry. In each of the years 2014 through 2019, he was named one of America's Most Honored Professionals by the American Registry, which also named Mr. Krompier one of America's Most Honored Lawyers in 2020, 2021, 2022, 2023, and 2024. He also was identified as a Distinguished Attorney by Martindale-Hubbell each year from 2014 through 2024.

In addition, Mr. Krompier is a named expert in the field of medical and dental malpractice defense litigation by Worldwide Who's Who and in 2015 became a lifetime member of Trademark Who's Who, Honors Edition. In 2017, he was included in Worldwide Publishing's *Top Lawyers: The Secrets to Their Success.* In 2018, 2019, 2020, 2021, 2022, 2023, 2024, and 2025, Mr. Krompier was named one of America's Top 100 High Stakes Litigators for New Jersey and one of America's Top 100 Civil Defense Litigators for New Jersey. In 2021, 2022, 2023, 2024, and 2025, he also was named one of America's Top 100 Medical Malpractice Litigators for New Jersey.

Mr. Krompier is a member of the New Jersey Bar (1980) and the New York Bar (1988) and has been admitted to the US District Court for the District of NJ (1980) and the US Court of Appeals for the Third Circuit (1986). In 2021, Mr. Krompier was admitted to the Bar of the Supreme Court of the United States.

Mr. Krompier has defended over 750 malpractice lawsuits involving most medical and dental specialties and has served as defense counsel in more than 100 malpractice trials from jury selection through verdict.

This is Mr. Krompier's third book. In 2012, he published *Defense from Within: A Guide to Success as a Dental Malpractice Defense Expert* for dental professionals. In 2021, Mr. Krompier published *Power from Within: A Guide to Success as a Medical Malpractice Defense Expert* for medical providers.

Chapter 1

You've Been Served

A typical malpractice Complaint will recite the names of the parties and their addresses, the dates of treatment, the nature of the treatment provided, the alleged injuries, and the relief sought by the plaintiff/patient. Some jurisdictions, like New Jersey, do not require that the Complaint contain all the pertinent details of the matter but only enough information to put the defendant practitioner "on notice" of the existence of a claim with only some general details of that claim. Other states require that the Complaint reference all the necessary details supportive of the malpractice claim. Either way, the Complaint serves as the initiating document for the patient's claims and which will require the filing of an Answer with the court.

Damages

Routinely, the relief desired by a plaintiff in a malpractice case is compensatory in nature. That is, the plaintiff wants to receive monetary compensation for the injuries allegedly sustained by the negligent treatment you provided and/or as a

DOI: 10.4324/9781003459002-1

result of your failure to obtain the plaintiff's informed consent to treatment. The specificity of the Complaint will be dictated by state law. In some instances, the Complaint also seeks punitive damages. As will be discussed in later sections, this is monetary relief beyond the routine compensatory damages and if obtained is designed to punish you for conduct that is deemed egregious, i.e., willful, wanton, or malicious and/or which reveals an utter disregard for the health, safety, or well-being of your patient. Needless to say, it is truly the rarest of cases where such conduct exists and where such damages are awarded. It is important to understand that claims of negligence are covered by your malpractice insurance policy to the extent of your policy limit. Acts that give rise to punitive claims, in fact, are not insurable because your policy covers acts of negligence and does not apply to conduct which is considered willful or intentional.

Since Complaints that contain punitive damage claims combine such claims with those for compensatory damages, your insurance company likely will provide you with counsel and a defense from the outset with a reservation of rights indicating that, should there be a punitive award at trial, that award will not be paid by your insurance company. Instead, such an award will have to be paid by you from personal assets. You also will be advised that you can, and perhaps should, retain personal counsel to protect your personal assets to the extent that they are exposed and can be protected.

Alerting Your Carrier

It becomes your obligation to timely provide your professional liability insurance company with a copy of the Complaint directly or indirectly through your insurance agent. You should not "bury" the Complaint under other papers on your desk or "hide" it in your briefcase and forget about it. It will not go away on its own, and you have a contractual obligation under the terms of your insurance agreement to alert your malpractice carrier of the existence of the Complaint in a timely manner and to furnish a copy to the insurance company.

Once your insurance carrier receives the Complaint, it will assign an attorney from a panel of approved counsel to represent you. You will be notified of the assignment of counsel, and the attorney thereafter will contact you.

While waiting for that initial communication from your newly assigned lawyer, it is important to keep your emotions in check. You should not let the receipt of a malpractice Complaint interfere with your day-to-day responsibilities, personal, or professional. Although it may prove to be a distraction, don't let this occurrence consume you.

Do not spend any significant time replaying in your mind the events of treatment or the occurrence of conversations to identify the single event or conversation which you think may have been pivotal during the care of the plaintiff and which may have prompted the filing of a Complaint. There will be ample opportunity to discuss the subject events with your attorney in due course and their impact on the ultimate outcome of treatment.

Nor should you allow feelings of guilt or shame to creep into your psyche. Unless you already know with certainty that you were professionally negligent in your treatment of the plaintiff, you must maintain a positive attitude. "Guilt" is not a concept that has any application in the context of a civil lawsuit such as a malpractice matter. Guilt or innocence only exist in a criminal prosecution. You also might feel ashamed because you have been sued for malpractice. Shame also has no place. Unfortunately, the number of highly capable and incredibly competent practitioners who have become malpractice defendants is ever increasing, and it is not necessarily because they are poor physicians. Simply stated, there is no shame in being sued professionally. It is a somewhat regular occurrence in today's litigious society.

Finally, in moments of silence and solitude following the receipt of a malpractice Complaint, you may be tempted to reconsider who you are and why you do what you do. Remember that the reason you became a physician was to be of help to those in need. That one patient has seen fit, with the aid of an attorney, to seek compensation for alleged negligence should not cause you to rethink who you are or why you chose the professional path you did.

Chapter 2

Initial Response to Lawsuit

If treatment of the plaintiff involved office-based care, you likely will look at the chart and review the referenced events. That's to be expected. Reading the chart may possibly assist in your recollection of the patient and the care that is the subject of the suit. Nothing in the chart should be modified, even slightly. If you now see an error, big or small, leave it alone. Change nothing.

If any of the treatment occurred in a hospital or surgical center, do not access the medical record for any reason. Though you may be tempted to do so, await the guidance of your attorney about how to review the chart.

If the Complaint identifies other practitioners as defendants who you know personally or professionally, do not contact any of them. There should never be communications with anyone regarding the suit or the underlying facts other than those you will exchange with your attorney or representatives of your insurance carrier. Conversations with counsel or your carrier representative are privileged and will not be disclosed.

Invariably, your deposition will be conducted at some point during the litigation, as will that of the other defendants. It is expected that questions will be asked about conversations with the other defendants. Not knowing what you might discuss, it is feared that a comment could be unknowingly offered, inculpating yourself or others, and that you would then be forced to repeat the remark at deposition. The better response, when asked at deposition, is that you have not had any discussions with anyone.

Nor should you speak to non-party colleagues about the matter. Again, there is no reason to discuss the suit or your treatment giving rise to the suit with anyone other than your counsel or your carrier representative. Even if you feel peace of mind dictates the need to chat with other practitioners about the case, resist doing so. For the same reason, you should not speak to other defendants in the matter; talking to professional colleagues is a bad idea.

You also may want to conduct a literature search, online, or otherwise. Don't. If literature is needed, as may be determined by your attorney, only then should a search be performed. Should your attorney want you to provide relevant literature, you will be so directed. Your counsel will discuss the best way to prepare a defense and whether identifying literature should be part of that effort.

Chapter 3

Your Defense Counsel

Within a few days of receipt of a Summons and Complaint, you should notify your insurance agent or insurance carrier directly, as is your obligation pursuant to the terms of your policy. You will be directed to forward copies of the suit papers and to provide copies of your treatment records. Of course, nothing in the chart should be modified or amended. Upon reviewing the treatment notes, you may conclude that omissions exist and, in the interest of completeness, be tempted to add information. Resist the temptation. There absolutely is no reason to modify any portion of the record, even if you believe clarity or completeness dictates the need for changes.

Typically, the carrier representative will briefly discuss the treatment in issue and respond to basic questions about what lies ahead. Soon thereafter, you will be advised of the assignment of a defense attorney, and you will receive the attorney's contact information. Once the selected lawyer has been advised of the assignment, counsel will communicate with you. Of course, if you have not heard from your attorney within two weeks of your communication with your

DOI: 10.4324/9781003459002-3

insurance carrier or insurance agent, certainly you can initiate communication.

As a matter of routine, you can expect that defense counsel will advise you in writing of his or her representation of you. A request will be made for a copy of your Curriculum Vitae. An initial telephone conversation thereafter likely will ensue during which your attorney will describe counsel's role on your behalf and the initial process of preparing and filing an Answer to the Complaint. Your lawyer will request a complete color copy of your office records and photographs, as well as any radiographs or imaging studies. Patient registration/intake forms, billing records, and other documents in your practice's computer system also will be requested. Your attorney will want to meet with you either in person or via Zoom, which meeting likely should take place within 30–60 days of the initial phone conference.

Chapter 4

Initial Meeting with Defense Counsel

It is expected that your first encounter with counsel will occur after your chart and related records have been reviewed by your attorney. Consequently, a portion of the time will be devoted to a discussion about the contents of those documents as well as your recollection of the plaintiff. In essence, the facts will be fully explored. Some time will be devoted to a review of the allegations contained in the Complaint so that responses can be drafted and included in the Answer to be filed with the court. Invariably, your attorney will deny all claims of negligence asserted in the Complaint.

If you provided copies of your office records to your attorney in advance of the meeting, as you should, be prepared to discuss them in some detail. Presumably, the chart will serve as a roadmap of the treatment received by the plaintiff and will allow for an organized discussion of your care. Be receptive to questions posed by counsel about your treatment recommendations and your recollection of conversations with the plaintiff, plaintiff's family members, if any, and other treaters who also may be defendants in the case.

DOI: 10.4324/9781003459002-4

To the extent that the Complaint includes a lack of informed consent claim, expect questions from your counsel as to the viable options to the treatment provided and whether those alternatives, including the option of non-treatment, were disclosed to the plaintiff. As you should know, it is required that a meaningful discussion with any patient about viable medical or surgical treatment options must also include disclosure of the material risks and benefits of each alternative. To the extent that your chart recites such conversations with the plaintiff, counsel likely will probe the details of those discussions. Certainly, the existence of a signed Consent Form will prompt questions by counsel about the circumstances surrounding the presentation and execution of that document by the plaintiff. If the Consent Form contains the signature of a witness, as it should, anticipate questions about the identity of that individual and the role the witness played in the consent process.

In some instances, a nurse, medical assistant, or other staff member will hand the Consent Form to a patient to read while the staff member watches the patient read the document. In other situations, the witness will not watch the patient read the Consent Form but will merely observe the signing of the document. In certain circumstances, the witness is present while the physician explains the subject treatment and answers questions posed by the patient. The protocol of the office certainly will be discussed at the meeting.

Although it may not occur at the initial conference, you will be expected to identify the names of your office employees who may have interacted with the plaintiff and who may have some pertinent recollection of the plaintiff. You should resist engaging in a substantive conversation with your staff other than to learn who recalls the plaintiff. Then, the individuals' contact information should be furnished to your counsel so that he or she can arrange a meeting.

If your treatment of the plaintiff involves hospital care, you can expect that your counsel will obtain copies of the chart with a HIPAA-compliant executed Authorization which the plaintiff's lawyer is obligated to provide to your lawyer. If the hospital is a party, hospital counsel will provide a copy of the chart to your attorney. Understand that once the plaintiff has placed his or her treatment in issue by filing a lawsuit, counsel for the various hospital and individual defendants are permitted to exchange the plaintiff's medical records without first obtaining an executed Authorization. Expect that all records secured by your attorney will be supplied to you for review and comment.

Do not obtain copies of hospital records yourself, even if the chart is part of an Electronic Medical Record (EMR) system that allows you access. Unless directed otherwise by your attorney, it is always preferable to have counsel secure records for you. As you can appreciate, an Audit Trail is part of the EMR. Routinely, plaintiffs' attorneys seek and obtain Audit Trails. If you are found to have accessed the chart after the filing of a suit, expect to field questions at your deposition about the reason you did so. Given that the plaintiff no longer is a patient of that hospital, there really is no reason to review the EMR, so the thinking goes. Suspicion may also be aroused about the purpose of such access when treatment is long over. Could it be because you want to modify some of your chart entries? Likely not, but there is no reason to put yourself in a position at deposition of having to explain your actions.

The meeting with counsel will also involve a discussion about your credentials. If you have a Curriculum Vitae (CV), send it to your counsel. If you do not have a CV, it is recommended that one be prepared. You should appreciate that a resume is not a CV. A resume typically is used in support of an application for employment and contains self-serving and subjective commentary about the applicant's unique skill set and career goals. Embellishment of one's professional accomplishments is often found in a resume. It might also include detailed narratives of the various duties and responsibilities in prior positions. Simply put, a resume is not a Curriculum Vitae and cannot serve as a substitute for a CV. If you supply a resume, expect it to be modified by your attorney so as to make it a true CV.

The contents of a Curriculum Vitae will be addressed in detail below. But for now, understand that it is a document that should recite your education, training, and experience as well as practice affiliations, hospital privileges, board certifications, publications, presentations, professional societies, and academic positions, all without editorial comment. The CV serves multiple purposes in litigation. The CV is a simple way to inform your attorney about your credentials and can be referenced, when necessary, by counsel during the litigation. Invariably, your attorney will need to supply information about your professional background to opposing counsel as part of a discovery obligation. Forwarding a CV is a simple and effective way for your lawyer to furnish that information. It also is expected that adverse counsel will seek your deposition, at which time questions will be asked about your credentials. If the plaintiff's attorney already has your Curriculum Vitae, that part of the deposition will be shortened. Of course, it can serve as a jumping-off point for questions about your background, but that portion of your deposition will be shorter than it otherwise would be if adverse counsel did not have your CV. Your Curriculum Vitae also will be supplied by your attorney to any expert retained on your behalf and likely will be considered at the time the expert drafts a report.

It is not unusual to have been a malpractice defendant in the past, perhaps on multiple occasions. Unfortunately, such is the life of a practitioner. There is no shame in having been sued. All too often, highly educated, well-trained and experienced providers who are competent, capable, and skilled in their profession find themselves embroiled in malpractice lawsuits. Expect your attorney to ask about your prior experiences. If you have been a defendant in the past, counsel likely will spend less time reviewing the discovery process and all that lies ahead. If you have little to no memory of your prior lawsuit or have never previously been a malpractice defendant, significant time will be devoted to describing the process and your participation in the different stages of discovery.

If you are or have been the subject of investigation or inquiry by your state's licensing board, you need to advise your attorney. To the extent that you recall the details of any board matter, disclose them to counsel as well as the outcome unless the matter is still pending. Some usual board orders include making payment of a fine to the board, returning fees to the complaining patient, reimbursing the insurance company for fees paid to you, directing participation in specified continuing education courses, and, rarely, license suspension. Although board matters inclusive of hearings before the board are quite different than malpractice suits and trials, it's important to educate your lawyer about all your experiences.

Your attorney will describe the discovery process to you and the degree to which you will be an active participant in that process. Your cooperation is key, as is your willingness to assist in your own defense, as will be discussed below.

Chapter 5

Basic Discovery

No matter the state in which you practice, the time between
the filing of an Answer to the Complaint with the court and
the ultimate resolution of the matter will be used by your
counsel to gather and supply information in furtherance of
your defense. The term "discovery" is defined simply as the
process of securing facts from the adverse party in a number of specified ways as permitted by the court rules of the
jurisdiction in which the lawsuit is pending. In the end, the
process is designed to facilitate the exchange of information
so that the parties are ready for trial. The added benefit to the
full exchange of information is the avoidance or elimination of
trial surprises. The sequence of discovery typically is dictated
by the local Rules of Court of the state in which the suit has
been filed. But most jurisdictions allow for discovery in much
the same way.

   The discovery process involves various methods of gathering information from the plaintiff's attorney and the attorney
representing any co-defendant. Of course, your counsel is
obligated to provide information as well. The methods utilized
for the gathering of information are identified by the Rules of
Court of the jurisdiction in which the suit is venued, but are

                      DOI: 10.4324/9781003459002-5

similar from state to state. The two most basic and frequently used discovery tools are interrogatories and depositions.

Interrogatories

It is typical for the parties to initially seek written answers to written questions. Those questions are routinely termed "interrogatories" and the responses are referenced as "answers to interrogatories". Interrogatories will seek some basic demographic information. Questions which you likely will need to answer will focus on the location and nature of your practice, your professional credentials, your contact with the plaintiff, the type and dates of treatment provided to the plaintiff, the identity of individuals who may have knowledge of any of the pertinent facts including eyewitnesses as well as those who may have made statements or admissions about relevant suit-related matters, the identity of possible trial witnesses including experts, and a somewhat detailed chronology of events. The interrogatories will ask you to identify the existence of any applicable professional liability insurance policies, the insurance coverage limits, coverage periods, and the policy numbers. If you have a CV, as you should, your counsel will attach it to your interrogatory answers before they are provided to the plaintiff's attorney. You will need to identify your office records, and a complete copy of your office chart and computer-based documents will be furnished to the plaintiff's attorney. Typically, you will be asked whether your license to practice has ever been suspended, revoked, or terminated in any state. If you have been the subject of a state licensing board investigation, you will need to provide that information. If convicted of a crime, that information will be furnished.

A detailed disclosure of other malpractice actions will be sought, including the allegations, the names of the plaintiffs, the identity of the court where the other matters were filed, the applicable docket numbers, and the way the cases were resolved or whether any are still pending. If you referred the plaintiff to other providers, you will be asked to identify such individuals as well as the reason for the referrals. If you maintain that the plaintiff is somehow responsible for the alleged injuries that are the subject of the Complaint, you will need to explain the basis for such a claim. Similarly, if it is your position that a third party caused the plaintiff's alleged injuries in whole or in part, the identity of that third party will need to be disclosed.

Importantly, the preparation of interrogatory answers is a process that requires the collaboration of client and counsel. You likely will be asked by your attorney to prepare draft responses to the interrogatories served by the plaintiff's lawyer. After doing so, expect that your attorney will modify your preliminary answers. If your responses are shortened, don't be surprised or offended. Routinely, defendants provide more information than is needed in interrogatory answers. You likely will be no exception. It is your attorney's obligation, based on education and experience, to tailor your answers in a way that the requested information is provided without extraneous or unnecessary comment. If you are uncomfortable drafting rough answers to the interrogatories, inform your attorney. An initial set of draft responses will be prepared for your review and approval. Of course, finalized answers will require your review and acceptance.

You will see that some of the interrogatories seek information that is best provided by your counsel. By way of example, questions that seek the basis for a legal defense as asserted in the Answer filed on your behalf cannot possibly be answered by you. Expect your attorney to draft responses to such interrogatories and to explain the basis for the answers. Of course, final responses to all questions will require your approval. You will then be obligated to sign and date a Certification which recites that the answers are true and accurate. Your certified interrogatory responses will then be forwarded to the plaintiff's attorney with a complete copy of your office records, if applicable, as well as a copy of your CV.

The obligation to provide discovery is a universal one. All parties, including the plaintiff, are required to provide interrogatory answers. As are you, the plaintiff must also supply pertinent and relevant documents in response to your counsel's formal written demand, which will be sent to the plaintiff's attorney. Each jurisdiction has published Rules of Court that establish time frames for providing interrogatory answers and responses to a request for the production of documents. Although all counsel strive to comply with the applicable Rules of Court, there are times when extensions are needed for a variety of reasons. Attorneys generally are willing to accommodate an adverse counsel's need for additional time, and the impact on the timely completion of discovery is rarely an issue. If deadline dates are addressed by the court in a Court Conference or in response to a motion filed with a judge, leniency in the enforcement of strict deadlines is somewhat routine.

Depositions

Following the exchange of interrogatory answers and responses to document demands, depositions of the parties are scheduled. Routinely, the plaintiff's deposition occurs first, and the defendant's deposition is taken thereafter. If the matter involves multiple defendants, the sequence of the various defendant depositions is somewhat random and dependent on the schedules of the individual defendants. There are times, however, when the plaintiff's attorney will schedule the defendants' depositions in a certain order to secure information from one defendant before that defendant can be influenced by the deposition testimony of another defendant. A court reporter will be present at each deposition, and a transcript will be prepared and forwarded to each attorney. You can expect your attorney to supply you with a copy of each deposition transcript for your review. An in-depth discussion of the deposition stage of discovery will be found in a later chapter.

As for securing the deposition testimony of the plaintiff's family members or friends, your counsel will ask the plaintiff's attorney whether such individuals can be voluntarily produced for deposition without subpoenas. No one welcomes having a process server appear at the door with a subpoena, and frequently a witness will agree to a deposition without being forced to testify in response to a subpoena.

Essential Discovery Goals

The purpose of discovery is to secure pertinent information in furtherance of a claim or a defense. The timing varies from case to case and generally is controlled by counsel in accordance with the jurisdictions' applicable Rules of Court. You need not concern yourself with how quickly or how slowly discovery progresses. The timetable of discovery is controlled to a significant degree by your attorney, who will move the process forward in a manner that best protects you and furthers your defense. Your role in that process will be disclosed by your lawyer at the outset, and no matter the speed at which discovery progresses, that role will not change. As noted above, you will be a necessary participant in the discovery process in very defined ways, and the assistance you provide to your counsel may be key to a successful defense.

Chapter 6

The Three Bears

Every matter is different factually. However, with rare exception, discovery proceeds in much the same way in every case. What differs is the amount of time and effort you devote to the process. Defense counsel will welcome and encourage a malpractice defendant to be an integral participant in the defense effort. Although you can expect your counsel to be an experienced malpractice litigator, it is likely that your attorney has never practiced medicine. Consequently, the insight which you have gained largely because of your education, training, and experience should be shared with your lawyer.

As you can appreciate, the degree to which you actively participate in the process will be dictated by your counsel. This means that your attorney will identify the assistance from you that is needed. The nature of that aid may be different from one matter to another. However, your counsel is in the best position to recognize and articulate the need for input from you. As a general statement, it is undeniable that your careful review of treatment records supplied by counsel during the discovery process is essential to a fruitful defense. Your attorney will appreciate your ability to uncover and identify chart entries that will assist in the defense. Your review of the

DOI: 10.4324/9781003459002-6

plaintiff's interrogatory answers and deposition testimony may also uncover statements that can be of assistance. If found, share those discoveries with your attorney. Similarly, reading the interrogatory answers and deposition testimony of other defendants, if any, may prove helpful. You may see a remark by a co-defendant that favorably impacts your defense. Even if you're not certain as to whether your finds will be of help to your counsel, it never hurts to share them and allow your attorney to determine their value.

However, you should avoid bombarding your lawyer with repetitive emails, texts, and calls that do little to advance your defense. At some point, such conduct becomes counterproductive. Instead of helping counsel, your effort becomes distracting and disruptive. You may think that providing repetitive messages will serve the purpose of helping the remarks to "sink in". Although such an approach has some limited merit, generally it should be avoided.

Being a defendant who is detached from the process, however, is neither recommended nor desirable. Too often, a defendant will ignore documents supplied by counsel for reasons that can't be legitimately explained. Perhaps it is the product of you being a very busy practitioner. It should not be the result of a lack of interest in the process or the thought that counsel will take care of everything. Some defendants tend to think the insurance carrier assigned attorney can handle the matter and that active involvement is unnecessary. That thinking is flawed. Again, you should be guided by defense counsel's instructions and at no time should you ignore those directions. Nevertheless, all too often a defendant provides minimal input during discovery, and it is only at the time of getting ready for trial that the defendant discloses that little effort was devoted to the review of materials supplied by counsel during the discovery phase. Try not to be this defendant.

The point to be made is that your degree of involvement should represent a balance between apathy and obsession. Avoid doing little to nothing to assist counsel. But also avoid compulsive and unnecessary interference in the process by communications not invited nor recommended by your attorney. You can always ask your lawyer whether more is needed from you or whether less is warranted.

In sum, disruptive involvement is too much, apathetic disinterest is too little. As with the story of "The Three Bears", striking a comfortable and happy medium between these two extremes will always be considered just right.

Chapter 7

Additional Discovery Tools

In addition to the discovery methods already mentioned, there are other tools at counsel's disposal which may be utilized. The decision to use all, some or none of those tools will be dictated largely by case need to uncover specific information and overall discovery strategy.

Request for Party Documents

A frequently used discovery tool is a formal written request for the production of documents. Each party's attorney may serve on adverse counsel a demand for copies or if necessary originals of specifically identified documents. On the defense side, your lawyer likely will seek copies of photos of the plaintiff which refer or relate to the claimed injuries, the plaintiff's writings, emails, and/or texts exchanged with you or any other party, relevant audio recordings, treatment records, invoices, bills or statements, diaries, notebooks, logs, or calendars in the plaintiff's possession. Your lawyer also will seek pertinent

 DOI: 10.4324/9781003459002-7

documents from any co-defendant's attorney. Once received from your counsel, review all the items supplied and provide any input you think might be appropriate.

Non-Party Interviews and Depositions

The pursuit of discovery may require your attorney to seek an interview and/or deposition of someone who is not a party. These non-party witnesses may include other treaters, the plaintiff's family members or friends, or professional colleagues. Work superiors or co-workers of the plaintiff may also be subject to an interview or deposition. No one is required by law to voluntarily submit to an interview or deposition. However, if a voluntary interview cannot be secured, a witness can be subpoenaed for deposition. Frequently, both practitioners and lay individuals resist providing information in a voluntary informal setting. Only after receipt of a subpoena will such a person provide testimony. Many have an established procedural mechanism for a treater to discuss a patient's care short of deposition. With an appropriate HIPAA-compliant Authorization signed by the plaintiff and provided to your counsel by the plaintiff's attorney, the informal interview allows a defense lawyer to ask questions of a provider absent the presence of the plaintiff's attorney. That process can be telephonic, in person, or virtual. In most jurisdictions, a plaintiff's lawyer may seek an order from the court granting permission to participate in the interview. If the Court rules that the plaintiff's lawyer may appear and consequently your attorney decides against the informal interview, recourse is to conduct the questioning in a formal manner, i.e., deposition. Of course, with a deposition, a court reporter attends, and the witness's sworn testimony is reduced to transcript form. In some instances, the creation of a deposition transcript is preferable to its absence, as would be the case with an informal interview. As you might understand, potentially skewed notes taken by an attorney at an interview cannot be used to legally memorialize the witness's statements for use at trial. One can only effectively confront a treater about statements made in response to questioning with a certified transcript created by a court reporter at a deposition. Some lawyers will conduct a deposition rather than an informal interview so that helpful sworn comments contained in a deposition transcript can be used during discovery moving forward or at trial. Such a strategy may be considered after a court ruling permitting a plaintiff's attorney to attend an informal interview to be conducted by your counsel or for other reasons.

To the extent necessary, a plaintiff's lawyer can speak to a treater about some aspect of the plaintiff's care or condition without first advising your attorney. As you might appreciate, the interests of the plaintiff's lawyer and the plaintiff's treater are arguably aligned. They both share a duty to the plaintiff.

It is important to appreciate that a plaintiff's treater typically is not required by law to agree to an informal interview sought by defense counsel even with permission from the patient. In fact, many practitioners believe that it's in their patient's best interest to resist voluntarily offering treatment information. The importance of gathering information from a treater as determined by your lawyer will dictate strategy after a treater refuses an informal interview. If it is deemed essential to your defense, expect that counsel will consider a deposition. If it is anticipated that the deposition will do more harm than good, it will not be taken.

As for securing the testimony of the plaintiff's family members or friends, your counsel will ask the plaintiff's attorney whether such individuals can be voluntarily produced for deposition without subpoenas. No one welcomes having a process server appear at the door with a subpoena, and frequently a witness will agree to a deposition without being forced to testify in response to a subpoena.

Securing Non-Party Records

Similarly, your attorney will obtain treatment records from non-party providers with executed HIPAA-compliant Authorizations which the plaintiff's lawyer is obligated to provide. By filing suit, a plaintiff places his or her treatment in issue, thereby permitting the defense to obtain charts and records from those the plaintiff consulted and those who provided care of any type.

Pharmacy records may also be obtained by your attorney with the use of an executed Authorization or in response to a subpoena. Medications dispensed by a pharmacy may well be important to some aspect of your defense. By way of example, a plaintiff may claim psychiatric damage because of alleged negligent care warranting psychiatric counselling. Yet, a review of the plaintiff's medication profile reveals that psychiatric medications were prescribed and dispensed prior to the alleged negligence, thereby suggesting that the purported psychiatric injury predated and is unrelated to the treatment in issue. Expect to receive such pharmacy records for your review.

If a plaintiff claims that an alleged injury has impacted the plaintiff's employment status in some way, a release for the production of the plaintiff's employer's personnel file will be prepared by your lawyer and furnished to adverse counsel for execution by the plaintiff. Once received, your attorney will forward the release to the plaintiff's employer for the employment records. In the alternative, your counsel can serve the plaintiff's employer with a subpoena seeking the production of the plaintiff's personnel file. All too often, a plaintiff will advance a lost wage claim and/or allege that a treatment-related injury has somehow impacted job performance. Frequently enough, employment records do not support such allegations. For example, formal performance reviews in the plaintiff's personnel file may reveal that the plaintiff's supervisor has favorably remarked about the plaintiff's job competence and work-related accomplishments, leading to a wage or salary increase. Promotions referenced in the personnel file might belie a claim that the plaintiff has been adversely impacted at work by your treatment. As with other materials obtained by your counsel, such documents likely will reveal their value to your defense.

Review of Social Media

Clearly, social media has become an increasingly popular way of disclosing and discussing life's events, whether good or bad. Oftentimes, the plaintiff's experiences leading to the filing of a lawsuit are found on Facebook or other social media platforms. To the extent that a review of that part of a plaintiff's Facebook which is not private references treatment or suit-related topics, there may be information valuable to your defense.

Again, you can expect your counsel to share all social media posts obtained during discovery. As with all other discovery materials secured by your attorney, you should read such items and comment about anything of significance.

Chapter 8

Your Curriculum Vitae

Early in the litigation process, as noted above, your attorney
will ask for a Curriculum Vitae (CV). Before transmitting it,
confirm your CV's accuracy and make certain that it is current.
An old or outdated Curriculum Vitae is only minimally helpful to your lawyer. Understand that a defendant's CV is used
for a variety of purposes. It will educate your attorney about
who you are professionally, and it likely will be furnished to
other counsel during the discovery process. Its impact on the
plaintiff's attorney cannot be underestimated. Your credentials may be so impressive that adverse counsel would have
to take notice. I am not suggesting that, upon reading your
CV, the plaintiff's lawyer will recommend dismissal of the
suit. However, I am certain that a well-prepared and complete
Curriculum Vitae, as a reflection of your professional stature,
will serve to enhance your credibility as a deposition witness and, more importantly when you testify before a jury.
At trial, your lawyer will elicit testimony from you about your
credentials as referenced in your Curriculum Vitae, and jurors
undoubtedly will consider those credentials, among other factors, in determining the weight to be given to your testimony.

DOI: 10.4324/9781003459002-8

With so much riding on the CV, it behooves you to make it as effective as possible.

Importantly, a CV is not a resume. The latter typically is used to support an application for a job, position, or privileges and, therefore, routinely contains personal information, self-serving comments about special skills and areas of expertise, as well as descriptions of certain professional experiences, none of which should be contained in a CV. Resist the temptation to give your lawyer a resume rather than a Curriculum Vitae. If you don't have a CV, prepare one. The time required to create a Curriculum Vitae is well worth the effort. If not fully familiar with the contents of an effective CV, consider the following recommendations.

In addition to listing your name, practice phone number, and professional email and mailing addresses on the top of the first page, your Curriculum Vitae should contain the following information.

Education and Training

List the names and locations of all schools attended after high school. Unless your high school was regionally or nationally famous, its inclusion is unnecessary. Indicate the years of attendance at or years of graduation from undergraduate, graduate, and post-graduate schools. Identify special education programs you attended and significant scholastic honors and awards you received. Internships, residencies, and fellowships should be mentioned. Include the nature, years, and locations of your training. Again, if you received special recognitions, honors, or awards during your training, your CV should recite them.

Board Certification

If you are board certified, list the name of the specialty board, the year of certification, and the year(s) of re-certification, if applicable. I don't typically recommend listing board eligibility only because it serves to highlight the fact that you are not board certified.

Hospital Affiliations

Identify all hospitals with which you currently are affiliated. List hospital names and locales, the nature of your privileges if other than full attending, and years of affiliation. Institutions with which you were associated in the past can be included if the termination of your privileges did not result from adverse action taken by the hospital. For example, if you moved your practice or voluntarily decided to limit the number of hospitals where you work for your convenience or to enhance patient care, identifying hospitals (with years of affiliation) where you no longer have privileges is acceptable. Particularly important positions held at hospitals also should be included in your CV. Department or division chair, chief, or director posts with years of service should be listed. So should significant hospital committee memberships or offices (with years of service) be included.

Academic Positions

A practicing clinician with an academic background is attractive to jurors. Consequently, if you teach or have taught, your CV should include your academic experience. Identify the institution by name and location, your position, and years of service.

Professional Organizations

Include all professional organizations, associations, and societies with which you are affiliated. Membership in defunct organizations or those to which you no longer belong typically should not be listed. If you hold or have held an important position in an organization, identify it and the years of service.

Military Experience

If you have served or currently serve in a branch of the military, National Guard, or Reserves, absolutely include this information. As a general statement, jurors respect the military, and, as one who has served or continues to serve, you will likely gain immediate respect from the jury. If you have served in a war theater or have seen military action, your stature will be further enhanced. If you have provided medical care during a war, this fact also should be reflected in your CV. Include significant decorations received from the military as well.

Awards and Honors

Professional citations of almost any type are worth mentioning in your CV. List the nature of the award or honor, the name of the entity that bestowed it, and the year of receipt. If a brief description of the accolade would help a layperson understand its significance, include it.

Publications, Presentations, Seminars and Lectures

Especially attractive are works that you have published, presentations to other practitioners, and seminars and lectures given on professional topics. Listed publications should include books, book chapters, articles, and abstracts. Full titles of the publications and publication years should be included. Presentations, seminars, and lectures similarly should be identified, inclusive of dates.

Athletic Program Affiliations

If you have held or hold a position with an athletic program or sports franchise, you are wise to identify it. For example, an association with a professional, semi-professional, college, or even high school sports team is valuable. If you are the podiatrist for a soccer team, the orthopedist for a football team, or the chiropractor for a gymnastics team, you may be accorded credibility by those jurors who support the team or the sport and perhaps by those who don't. After all, you must truly be an expert in feet and ankles if you are the podiatrist for an entire soccer team. So the thinking goes.

Public Service

By its very designation, this type of credential is impressive to jurors. Therefore, if you have served the public in some fashion, your CV should reflect it. For example, if you participate in school-sponsored programs, mention it. If you have participated in the local police department's D.A.R.E. (Drug Abuse Resistance Education) program by teaching children about the impact drugs have on the body, include it. An ophthalmologist who conducts free annual eye exams provides a valuable public service. Again, your public-mindedness will be well received by jurors and will tend to enhance the impression that you are "high-minded" and therefore reliable.

Media Appearances

Invited guest appearances on television, radio programs, or podcasts are also worth including in your CV. If you hosted such programs, all the better. Like service to a sports team, your participation in such programming suggests that you have been selected because you are particularly capable. Such appearances will promote the perception that you are a distinguished member of your profession.

Chapter 9

Answering Interrogatories

There are two notable ways in which your participation in discovery will be required. The first involves the preparation of written responses to written questions, typically referred to as interrogatories. The second involves providing testimony at a deposition, the details of which will be addressed below. As a matter of routine, your attorney will supply you with interrogatories, which the plaintiff's lawyer has provided, or which another defendant's attorney has supplied, or which your jurisdiction's Rules of Court require you to answer. Although your counsel will assist in writing final responses, you may be asked to prepare initial draft answers to some of the questions. The preparation of answers likely will be based on your memory, the review of relevant records, routine, habit, custom, or practice, or some combination of the above. Once your counsel reads and edits your answers, they will be forwarded to you for final review and acceptance. Some of the interrogatories will seek information only your attorney can legitimately answer on your behalf. Importantly, lawyers involved

DOI: 10.4324/9781003459002-9

in litigation understand and accept that a party's interrogatory responses are the result of a collaboration between counsel and client. Of course, at the end of the process, you will be asked to certify the truthfulness and accuracy of the responses.

As a general statement, interrogatory answers should be brief and direct. Unnecessarily long-winded and meandering responses should be avoided. To the extent other counsel may want more detail as it relates to any topic referenced in the interrogatory answers, questions will be asked at your deposition seeking elaboration.

Interrogatories generally seek information about your credentials, your practice, your involvement in the care of the plaintiff, and applicable insurance coverage. Expect your attorney to attach your Curriculum Vitae to your interrogatory answers before sending them to other counsel so as to eliminate the recitation of such information in those answers. If the matter involves informed consent claims, the interrogatories likely will include questions about the risks, benefits, and treatment alternatives disclosed to the plaintiff. If you reviewed treatises, texts, or professional journals in providing treatment to the plaintiff, you will be asked to identify them. Similarly, if you consulted colleagues while providing care to the plaintiff, identifying those individuals will be necessary. Referrals to other providers during treatment of the plaintiff will require the disclosure of their names.

The identity of individuals who may have relevant knowledge will also be sought. You likely will need to disclose pertinent records and documents of which you are aware. For example, your responses should reference treatment and billing records that pertain to the plaintiff as well as imaging studies. To the extent that such documents are in your custody and/or control, copies will have to be supplied to your counsel so that they can be attached to your interrogatory answers before transmittal to other counsel. Some jurisdictions require you to prepare and provide a typed transcription of handwritten entries in the treatment records. As you may appreciate, there is no legitimate reason why other parties should have to decipher your handwriting.

Relevant statements and admissions made by third parties to you, or which you have made to third parties, should be identified. If those statements or admissions are in written form, inclusive of letters, emails, or texts, copies should be furnished to your lawyer. They then will be supplied by your attorney with your interrogatory answers. If you believe that the plaintiff's alleged injuries were the result of the actions of others and/or those of the plaintiff, a statement to that effect should be included in your interrogatory responses. At times, it may be appropriate to reference another event, like a previous motor vehicle accident or one which post-dates the subject treatment, as the cause of the plaintiff's claimed injuries. It may also be proper to identify an underlying condition as the cause of or contributory to the claimed injuries. To the extent that you are aware of witnesses to any of the subject events or conversations, they should be mentioned. Audio or video recordings of any pertinent matter must also be identified and produced.

In many jurisdictions, interrogatories will request the identity and credentials of proposed experts. Where the local Rules of Court obligate the parties to respond, this information will be supplied by your counsel and can be contained in your answers. Since interrogatory answers are routinely provided early in the discovery process, your lawyer may recommend a "to be supplied" response to this and various other questions that seek information prematurely. In some venues, there is no obligation to identify with specificity those who may serve as experts. As a result, no expert witness information will be included in your interrogatory answers.

If you have ever been the subject of investigation by your state's licensing board, questions about that experience may be asked. To the extent you have been a malpractice defendant in the past or are currently involved in a pending matter, you will be expected to provide that information.

Chapter 10

Your Deposition

The second and arguably most important aspect of discovery in which you will be required to actively participate is your deposition. As you may already know, a deposition is a live session, in which the plaintiff's attorney will question you in the presence of your counsel about the events that have given rise to the suit. You will be asked to take an oath and swear or affirm that you will provide truthful testimony. Prior to COVID-19, almost all party depositions were conducted in person in the office of the attorney representing the individual being deposed. During COVID-19, nearly all depositions were taken remotely, with all participants in different locations, including the court reporter whose purpose it is to steno-graphically record your sworn testimony. Since COVID-19, the practice of remotely conducting depositions has routinely continued as a matter of convenience. There is no traveling involved and you can comfortably testify from your office or home. Although your attorney may not be physically by your side, protection of your interests is not sacrificed by counsel's remote participation. Oftentimes, the plaintiff's lawyer will video-record your testimony, which video recording can be used at the time of trial in a number of ways. Regardless, your

DOI: 10.4324/9781003459002-10

testimony should not be affected. Nor should your attire. You should always dress professionally whether your deposition is video-recorded or not.

Demeanor is key. You should not be arrogant, impatient, combative, or condescending. As offensive as the process may seem or as unsettling as the deposition may be, always maintain your composure. Focus on the questions posed and remain mindful of your lawyer's pre-deposition instructions. Always provide reasonable and reasoned responses.

Your Counsel's Role

It is your lawyer's obligation to object to questions that are improper and to direct you to not answer questions that in the extreme should not be asked in the first place. For example, a question that is unclear or which incorporates language that may be subject to varying interpretations may be difficult if not impossible to answer. Should your lawyer object to such a question because of the form, the questioning attorney might opt to rephrase the question to make it understandable. A question to which your attorney objects based on its form should still be answered if you understand it. Of course, upon hearing that your lawyer has an objection, the questioning attorney may choose to rephrase the question. Importantly, if you understand a question notwithstanding your counsel's objection, you should provide a response. There may be times when the questioning lawyer asks a question that your attorney considers so improper that an objection is interposed, and you are instructed not to answer the question. Rarely asked questions that seek confidential or privileged information routinely are the subject of an objection and an instruction that you not answer the question. By way of example, a question that seeks information about your communications with counsel is absolutely improper. It intrudes upon the attorney-client privilege and should never be asked. If you hear such a question, you can expect your lawyer to object and to direct you not to answer.

Instructions

At the outset of the deposition, you will receive a series of instructions from the plaintiff's attorney that are designed to provide some basic guidance as to how to function. Typically, you will be advised to: (1) verbally respond to all questions posed; (2) avoid the use of nonverbal answers such as shrugs or head nods; (3) answer questions with words and not sounds such as "hmm" or "uhuh" or "nah"; (4) refrain from answering any question before it's fully stated; (5) avoid answering a question with a guess; (6) advise if a question is not understandable; (7) indicate if a break is needed at any time; and (8) remain silent if your attorney objects to a question, and then answer only after the objection is fully stated unless your lawyer directs you otherwise. You also will be told that, if you answer a question, it will be concluded that you heard and understood the question. Importantly, you likely will be asked whether you have conferred with your attorney about the nature and purpose of the deposition. It's expected that your answer will be in the affirmative, allowing the questioning lawyer to safely believe that you understand the process. Of course, you may wonder why the plaintiff's attorney is permitted to ask this question as it seems to intrude upon privileged attorney-client communications. In short, you are not being asked to disclose the substance of exchanges with your counsel. Rather, the plaintiff's lawyer is seeking to confirm that you understand the deposition process before it begins. That effort is permissible, and that single question is allowed. In theory, if you answer in the affirmative and, after the deposition is concluded, you attempt to place some distance between you and the testimony given by remarking that you don't understand why you were asked questions or the reason for the deposition in the first place, such comments will be of no legal significance. After all, you acknowledged your understanding of the deposition process before the deposition began.

You can expect that questions about your credentials, the nature of your practice, and the treatment provided to the plaintiff will be posed by the plaintiff's attorney. If other defendants are parties to the matter, their counsel will attend your deposition, and they may also ask questions. Your testimony will be given under oath, and all that is said at the deposition will be recorded by a court reporter or stenographer.

Routinely, the plaintiff's deposition is conducted first as it is the plaintiff who initiated the suit and who has levied claims against you and perhaps others. The depositions of the defendants will follow. The sequence of those depositions will be determined by the plaintiff's lawyer, who may have a scheme in mind for conducting all the defendants' depositions. It is quite possible that the order of the defendants' depositions may be rather random and dictated by the professional schedules of the various defendants.

Preparation

Your attorney likely will supply a copy of the transcript of each party's deposition taken before your deposition so that you can read what others have said. By doing so, you may read about aspects of treatment, events, or conversations that trigger your memory. You also may read about an aspect of treatment, an event, or conversation that you recall differently. Either way, there is value in reading what others, especially the plaintiff, have said.

In advance of your deposition, your counsel will schedule a pre-deposition meeting, the purpose of which is multifaceted. That conference should be scheduled on a date close enough to the actual deposition so that the instructions are easily recalled. However, that meeting should not be held so close to the deposition that last-minute adjustments to strategy cannot be implemented.

There will be a discussion about the status of discovery to date, significant entries in the treatment records obtained by counsel, salient portions of the plaintiff's deposition, as well as critical excerpts from the depositions of the co-defendants, if any. Whether you have given a deposition in the past or have no deposition experience, your attorney will counsel you as to how to conduct yourself and how to respond to anticipated questions.

The plaintiff's attorney will give you some basic instructions at the outset of your deposition as noted above, some of which may be repetitive of the guidance given by your lawyer at the pre-deposition meeting. You should adhere to the instructions provided by your counsel, which likely will include the following. You will be instructed to refrain from answering a question before hearing the entirety of the question. All too often, a witness will respond to a query before the entire question is posed. When that occurs, the witness may begin answering a question that is different than the question about to be asked. As a result, the witness volunteers information that is not being sought, prompting the questioner to restate the question. Worse yet, the unsolicited remarks may prompt the questioner to inquire about the information voluntarily supplied that otherwise would not have been the subject of a question. The secondary concern about speaking while the questioner is talking is that the court reporter who is duty-bound to record everything stated at the deposition will have difficulty hearing and accurately recording the remarks of two people speaking at once. As a result, the court reporter will ask the questioner and/or you to repeat what was stated or, worse yet, inaccurately record your testimony. Court reporters who are retained in malpractice matters are generally competent in hearing and accordingly recording technical terms and phrases that you may use at a deposition. With that said, there may be times when the court reporter will interrupt you in the middle of a response because there was difficulty hearing something said and ask you to repeat a portion of your testimony. Should that happen, do not be distracted by the interruption. Restate the inaudible remark and resume your testimony.

You will be instructed to avoid guessing, as a guess is not based on anything factual. Of course, you will be permitted to respond with an estimate or an approximation if appropriate. You should confine your responses to the questions being asked and refrain from offering gratuitous statements outside the scope of any question. Voluntary and unsolicited testimony does nothing to enhance your performance. Rather, it introduces extraneous information which was not sought and allows the questioner to pose additional queries that otherwise would not have been asked but for the voluntary testimony. Nor should you answer a question with a question. If you are somewhat confused about a question, simply state that you don't understand the question. You should not ask the attorney to clarify the question in some way. Rather, you should comment that the question is unclear. That will force the questioner to rephrase the question or ask a completely different question. In the alternative, the attorney may ask you to explain the reason why the question is not understandable, which explanation may then prompt a new question.

Adequate preparation also requires that you devote time on your own to the review of pertinent documents. Those materials necessarily include your chart, any applicable hospital records, and your interrogatory answers. Although you may have reviewed those documents at an earlier stage of the

litigation, you should refresh your recollection of their content
by reading them again. Should that review prompt questions
for your counsel, make certain that you speak to your attorney in advance of the deposition and do not leave anything to
chance. It is not uncommon for the plaintiff's attorney to ask
what materials you reviewed in preparation for the deposition.
Be prepared to answer that question by identifying those documents. A second and frequently asked question may focus
on other materials that you received from your attorney during the pendency of the case and which you have read. Those
documents may include the interrogatory answers of other
parties, transcripts of their depositions, records of other practitioners, and miscellaneous documents. Although you could
be asked questions about those materials, it is not recommended that you review those documents as part of deposition preparation. To do so is unnecessary. Devoting your time
to a review of all the materials supplied during the litigation
will be counterproductive. Your preparation time should be
focused on documents that bear on your involvement in the
plaintiff's care and your interrogatory answers. Simply stated,
if the plaintiff's attorney asks you questions about those materials and you have little or no recollection of their content,
such testimony will not adversely impact the quality of your
deposition or your overall defense.

Questions

At your deposition, you should expect to be asked questions
about your interrogatory answers. Consequently, make certain that the previously provided responses are as accurate
and correct at the time of deposition preparation as they were
at the time they were written. Of course, rarely should an
interrogatory answer reviewed months if not years later be
wrong. But it can happen, and before the erroneous response

is uncovered at your deposition, bring it to the attention of your lawyer in advance. In this way, a strategy as to how best to deal with the incorrect answer can be discussed and developed.

Also, expect questions to be asked about your education, training, and experience. Although your Curriculum Vitae previously supplied to the plaintiff's attorney will provide information about your credentials, the CV may well serve as a springboard to additional questions about your background. No one will expect you to recall all the details recited in your Curriculum Vitae, and for this reason, you likely will be permitted to look at your CV when answering questions about your credentials.

The deposition will focus on the nature of your practice at present and at the time of the subject treatment. Practice names, locations, and affiliations with other providers will be asked.

The focus of the deposition will transition to the actual care provided to the plaintiff. Although the plaintiff's lawyer may ask about your recollection of the treatment in question, no one would expect you to have a precise memory of the entire course of care. That your recall of all aspects of treatment may be imprecise or incomplete, few would expect otherwise. After all, your involvement in the plaintiff's care occurred years ago, and unless the plaintiff was your only patient, it is doubtful that you would be able to provide completely accurate and comprehensive testimony based on memory alone.

With the records of your treatment at hand, you will be permitted, if not encouraged to examine them in advance of providing an answer to a question. Frequently, with remote depositions, the plaintiff's counsel will "screen share" portions of the relevant records so that you and all participants can view them. If the deposition is conducted in person, "hard" copies of the records will be marked as deposition exhibits and made available to you.

Of course, if a claim has been made that your treatment records are incomplete, inadequate, or erroneous, expect questions about the preparation of your notes. For example, you may be asked whether they were entered at the time treatment was rendered or some time after treatment and whether they were intended to document all pertinent aspects of your enounter with the plaintiff. You may be asked whether your notes reference all treatment discussions. If you referred the plaintiff to another provider, expect a question about documentation of that referral.

Keep in mind that not all documentation omissions constitute a departure from the standard of care. Some might. Yet, it is generally understood that an inadequate note cannot directly cause injury to a patient, and therefore a malpractice claim based on documentation errors alone will not be successful. Of course, if a lack of informed consent allegation exists, documentation of the consent discussion may be critical to defending such a claim. If there is a signed consent form which contains all the pertinent information, however, the absence of a detailed note may not prove fatal to your defense.

Since you will be asked questions about past events, you will need to put yourself back in time, in a manner of speaking. Though your current thinking may be influenced by documents supplied by your counsel during the course of the litigation and/or conversations with counsel, you must divorce yourself from what you now know or your current thoughts. Your testimony should always be based on what you did, what you thought, what you heard, what you saw, and what you wrote in the record at the time treatment was provided to the plaintiff.

Understand that the ultimate issue is whether you complied with or deviated from the accepted standard of care. Unless you've disclosed otherwise to your lawyer, it is expected that your treatment of the plaintiff satisfied the standard of care.

Consequently, no matter when you are asked about that treatment, your testimony consistently will be that you acted in accordance with the standard of care.

It is possible that the plaintiff's attorney will ask whether one of the other defendants complied with the standard of care. Of course, such a question can be proper when the other defendant practiced in your discipline. You and your counsel should anticipate this question and should discuss your potential answer. If you thought at the time of treatment that the other defendants complied with the applicable standard of care, then answering such a question at deposition should not be problematic for you or the other defendants. If your thinking at the time of treatment, however, was that another defendant deviated from the standard of care, you must discuss with your lawyer at the pre-deposition meeting how best to address this topic.

As a general statement, a substantive answer may be based on your memory or the written record or some combination of the two. At the other end of the spectrum, you may have no recollection and are unable to provide a response based on the written record. In that instance, stating that you do not recall is an acceptable response. There is no shame in testifying that you do not remember something. If an "I don't remember" response is an honest answer, it does not matter how often you give that answer.

The middle ground testimony is that which is based on routine, habit, custom, or practice. For example, if you don't recall what you ate for breakfast one year ago today and there is no writing that assists in providing a response, your answer need not be "I don't remember". If your routine, habit, custom, or practice for the last two years has been to have a single cup of coffee and a piece of toast for breakfast, then you can confidently testify that a year ago today, you had a cup of coffee and a piece of toast for breakfast. When it serves your purpose to offer this kind of testimony rather than an "I don't recall" answer, then you should do so. Of course, this strategy should be discussed with your counsel in advance at the pre-deposition meeting. Keep in mind that a plaintiff's attorney can always ask whether you had a routine, habit, custom or practice as relates to some aspect of your care of the plaintiff, even if you do not invoke such a remark as part of an answer. Such a question is not unusual.

Importantly, you should never guess in response to any question. A guess is a response based on absolutely nothing factual. Avoid this temptation at all costs since guesswork can be your undoing. An estimation or approximation can be an appropriate answer when it is impossible to provide a more precise response. For example, you may not be able to state with certainty the number of patients you have seen in a given month in an identified year, but you might well be able to offer an approximate figure or an estimated number.

Of equal import, absolutely avoid offering gratuitous testimony. Always focus on the question before you and limit your answer to the topic raised. It serves no purpose to go beyond the scope of any question. Even the most talkative individual should recognize that voluntary testimony serves no purpose and can be counterproductive. Only address a question in a narrow way, as if wearing blinders. If you exceed the scope of a rather narrow question with a meandering, elongated response, bad things can happen. You might inadvertently offer information that could be damaging. You might say something that prompts the plaintiff's attorney to focus on a new area not previously contemplated, which itself can cause the deposition to take more time than otherwise necessary. Keep in mind that based on what was discussed at the pre-deposition meeting, your counsel will have a reasonable expectation as to the testimony you will be giving. If you deviate from that expectation, your attorney likely will be somewhat surprised and frustrated. There can be no advantage to volunteering information not sought by the plaintiff's lawyer.

Brevity is a virtue. Your answers should be short and to the point. If your answers are responsive, nothing more can be expected of you. The questioner can always pose follow-up queries if necessary. Let the plaintiff's counsel do the work of unearthing the information sought without your help in that effort. Your role is to answer the question before you and nothing more. In sum, less is more.

Of course, you should not be "cute" in your responses. By that, I mean, do not provide a deliberately short answer merely for the sake of being short when such an answer is not fully responsive. Also, avoid being evasive. Testify in a direct fashion. Evasiveness serves no purpose other than to prompt the plaintiff's lawyer to ask the same question again to secure responsive testimony, thereby prolonging the deposition. Repeatedly evasive testimony might not only frustrate the questioning attorney, resulting in an unnecessarily contentious proceeding, but it too may prompt the undeserved conclusion that you are a difficult individual and unpleasant practitioner.

Always wait to hear the full question before beginning your answer. You may be tempted to speak before the question is completely stated because you think you understand the question or because the phrasing or intonation of the questioner makes you believe the question has been fully stated, or some combination of the two. During everyday conversation, it is not unusual for people to talk over one another. This, however, is not a conversation. It is a deposition and therefore care must be taken to avoid the pitfalls that otherwise occur in our daily lives. As you will recall, I cautioned against volunteering information not being sought. Beginning an answer without first fully hearing the question likely will result in testimony not related to the question and the undesirable result that you have now volunteered unsolicited information.

There likely will be times when an unintelligible question is asked. It is not your job to interpret an unclear question. It is your job to answer clearly stated and understandable questions. Again, if you answer a question that you must first decipher, your interpretation may be mistaken, thereby leading to a response that is askew of the question's topic. Force the plaintiff's attorney to ask a clear question by simply stating that a question posed is not understandable. No one can expect you to answer a question you cannot comprehend.

Your attorney's role is to protect you and your interests at all stages of the litigation, including your deposition. The degree to which counsel can "run interference" depends on the local court rules. At a minimum, your lawyer will object to any question that is believed to be unclear and/or confusing. In such a situation, you must still provide an answer so long as you understand the question. In most jurisdictions, you must answer every understandable question posed even if your lawyer objects to the form of the question because it is unclear to counsel. That is, your lawyer cannot instruct you to not answer a question because counsel does not like the question. The touchstone is not whether your counsel comprehends the question but whether you understand it. However, it is not uncommon for both counsel and client to have difficulty comprehending a question. In the face of an objection to the form of a question, adverse counsel can rephrase the question to make it understandable or ask you why the question is unclear or move to another subject altogether. In most jurisdictions, as part of an objection to the form of a question, your attorney should not offer substantive comments to suggest how to respond or to otherwise prompt you.

If the case involves other defendants, their counsel may object to a question based on the question's form. Commonly, no speaking objection explaining the basis for the objection is permitted. Of course, you are not to be guided by the objections of other defense counsel. You should only focus on the objections, if any, made by your lawyer.

Some questions may attempt to seek confidential or privileged information. For example, should you be asked about any matter discussed with your attorney or your counsel's staff, your lawyer will object and direct you to not answer the question. Those communications are absolutely privileged, and you cannot be compelled to disclose such information at a deposition. As a further example, any question that intrudes into your personal finances inclusive of queries designed to elicit information about your annual salary or like compensation also will result in an objection by your attorney and an instruction that you not respond. In sum, any question at all that seeks confidential or privileged information may appropriately prompt an objection by your lawyer and an instruction that you not answer.

There are times when your attorney and adverse counsel may need to confer about a pending question that your lawyer finds objectionable. Those conversations should occur outside your presence so that you are not influenced by the comments of counsel. If your deposition is conducted live, you will be asked to leave the room while both counsel exchange thoughts about the question. If the deposition is being conducted remotely, you will be moved to a "break-out" room during counsels' discussion. Once the issue has been resolved, you will be invited back and the deposition will continue.

If the matter involves other defendants, their counsel may pose questions after the plaintiff's attorney finishes. As a general statement, other defendants' counsel typically will not ask questions unless your testimony in response to the plaintiff's lawyer's questions warrants the need to do so. If questions are asked, the rules that govern your conduct and that of your counsel are the same as when the plaintiff's attorney was conducting the examination.

It may occur that at the conclusion of questioning by the plaintiff's lawyer and other defense counsel, if any, your attorney asks questions. Do not be startled. It may be that the examination by other attorneys has resulted in a confused or unclear portion of the record, prompting the need for questioning by your lawyer to make that aspect of your testimony clear. The fact that your attorney has decided to pose questions does not mean that your testimony was lacking or otherwise problematic. It may simply mean that your counsel wanted to clarify the record.

Duration

A routine deposition of a defendant in a malpractice matter will vary in length. The factors that impact the duration include the complexity of the facts, the frequency and/or duration of treatment, the number of parties, and the medical issues. Attorneys who conduct depositions have different examination styles. Some lawyers are very efficient in their questioning and conduct relatively short depositions. Others spend more time examining a defendant, resulting in an extended proceeding. There is no right or wrong approach to taking a deposition. However, as a general statement, a defendant's deposition in a malpractice case likely will last between two and four hours. Some can be concluded in less than two hours, and some might last more than four hours. Your attorney likely will guide you as to the anticipated duration of your deposition.

No matter the length, you are entitled to take as many breaks during the deposition as you need. At any time, you can request a break and that request will always be granted. A break routinely can last anywhere from 5 to 15 minutes, but that range is not written in stone. A lunch break may last 20–30 minutes. Depending on the local court rules, you likely will be precluded from discussing your testimony, either that which you have given or that which you contemplate giving, with your attorney. Breaks are not intended to be an opportunity for you to confer with counsel about substantive matters. They are essentially comfort breaks. Of course, the presumption is that you have had ample time with your lawyer in advance of the deposition to address issues of substance.

In most jurisdictions, you cannot speak to your attorney during the deposition about how you might answer a question. You cannot ask for guidance in hushed tones while a question is pending. Nor can your counsel whisper advice.

Transcript

At some point after the deposition, a booklet of the proceeding will be prepared by the court reporter. That booklet, known as a deposition transcript, will contain all the questions and all your answers, as well as the objections or comments of your attorney and any other participating lawyers. The transcript usually is available two to three weeks after the deposition and is provided to all counsel. Once received, it will be forwarded to you to review. You should carefully read the entirety of the transcript and make certain that the court reporter has accurately recorded your testimony. You may find mistakes in the transcript based solely on your recollection of what you said and the language you recall using. You should read the transcript within a few days of receipt while the deposition is somewhat "fresh" in your mind. Of course, you cannot ask your attorney to have the court reporter change your testimony for any reason. If you have given an inaccurate or incorrect answer, it cannot be changed. If you wish you had used "better" language, you cannot ask that your response be replaced with different testimony. Only an error by the court reporter can be changed.

If a recording error exists, notify your lawyer as soon as possible so that counsel can advise the court reporter. In most venues, the court reporter then is obligated to check the stenographic notes and the audio recording to confirm the accuracy of the transcript or the legitimacy of the errors cited. If a mistake is found, the court reporter will issue a corrected transcript. The corrected transcript will be supplied to you by your lawyer for future reference, most notably in preparation for trial.

Chapter 11

Post Deposition Events

Additional Depositions

If the matter involves other defendants, the plaintiff's attorney likely will seek their depositions as well. As mentioned above, the sequence of conducting the depositions of all defendants will be dictated by the plaintiff's lawyer's discovery strategy and/or the professional schedules of the various defendants. If other defendants are deposed before your deposition is conducted, your lawyer likely will provide transcripts of their depositions. Of course, abide by your counsel's instruction as to whether you should read the transcript of any deposition before your deposition. You might benefit from reading the transcripts of the other defendants, as there may be testimony about events that are germane to your involvement in the plaintiff's care. Reading what others have said might provide insight that impacts your thinking. Of equal importance, the testimony of others might prompt a recollection of an event or conversation that you otherwise might not have remembered. You might also recall events in a manner much different than that of other defendants, and reading their depositions might force you to give thought to an issue that might not have

 DOI: 10.4324/9781003459002-11

commanded your attention. If you read something you believe to be remarkable, discuss it with your counsel.

Expert Reports

Once all party depositions are completed, discovery documents including deposition transcripts, interrogatory answers and pertinent medical, pharmacy and employment records, will be supplied by the plaintiff's counsel to experts retained on the plaintiff's behalf. Within a reasonable period thereafter, the plaintiff's lawyer will send to your attorney liability and/or causation and/or damages reports prepared by those experts. An expert report is written in the form of a formal letter, and its length is dictated by the nature of the case. If the matter is factually complex and/or encompasses complicated treatment issues, it is reasonable to expect that the report will be longer rather than shorter. As a general proposition, I have rarely seen a comprehensive expert report much less than three single-spaced typewritten letter-size pages. Even the simplest of matters likely will necessitate such a report. There are certain recognizable components of an expert report. They include reference to the materials reviewed, salient facts, treatment issues, opinions, the foundation for opinions, and ultimate conclusions. It is expected that the plaintiff's expert reports will identify deviations from the standard of care attributable to you, offer opinions causally connecting those deviations to the plaintiff's alleged injuries and recite the actual damages purportedly sustained by the plaintiff as result. Your attorney will supply the plaintiff's expert reports to you for review and will want your input. I strongly urge you to provide your thoughts in writing to your counsel within two to three weeks of receipt. In this way, your lawyer can reference your thinking repeatedly, if necessary, as the case continues to unfold. Indeed, your comments may be shared by your counsel with the defense experts retained on your behalf and may be a meaningful part of any dialogue your lawyer conducts.

Once your attorney receives the plaintiff's expert reports, they will be forwarded to the experts retained on your behalf along with discovery documents and pertinent records. You can expect your lawyer to identify individuals who are known experts in various practice areas and who are willing to assist in the defense of a malpractice matter. The components of a defense expert report will mirror those typically found in a plaintiff's expert report. The critical difference is that the defense expert report will state that your treatment was appropriate, that you did not deviate from the applicable standard of care and that any injury allegedly sustained by the plaintiff did not result from any act of negligence by you. After a defense expert report is received by your counsel, it will be provided to the plaintiff's attorney.

It is possible that you may be asked by your attorney if you know a practitioner who might be willing to serve as a defense expert. Such individual should have no relationship with you professionally or personally. The practitioner you identify should be known to you by reputation only, and perhaps because you have learned that the practitioner has served or is interested in serving as a malpractice expert. Any effort to contact such an individual should be made by your counsel only. You must not be involved in the process of communicating with any potential expert.

There are occasions, although few, when an expert opinion is unnecessary. For example, under the legal doctrine of *res ipsa loquitur*, which means literally "the thing speaks for itself", a jury may reasonably conclude that an alleged injury would not have occurred absent the defendant's misconduct. This doctrine rarely applies in malpractice matters because an expert opinion is almost always needed to address the propriety of what happened. Another exception to the liability expert opinion requirement exists where the "common knowledge" doctrine applies. Here, the law recognizes that there may be situations where lay individuals, based on their everyday experience, can determine if there has been a departure from the accepted standard of care. Application of this doctrine requires professional conduct so clearly wanting that it is obvious to a layperson.

By way of example, if right ear surgery is scheduled for a pediatric patient for mastoiditis and surgery is performed by a pediatric otolaryngologist, a less-than-optimal result may prompt the filing of a malpractice suit. If the surgery was neither ill-conceived nor improperly performed, there will be no basis for a malpractice action, unless, of course, the surgery was performed on the left ear instead of the right. Such was a case that I defended. As you might imagine, the plaintiffs did not retain an expert to address the issue of negligence. It was conceded that the problem ear was the right ear and not the left one. By surgically treating the wrong ear, the defendant practitioner clearly had deviated from the standard of care. The jury did not need, and the law did not require, the assistance of expert testimony to so find.

Interestingly, you would think that a case like this would have been settled rather than tried. After all, my client and I both understood that a trial would result in an adverse verdict. By eliminating the need to retain a liability expert, the plaintiffs (parents of the patient), through their lawyer, would be able to pursue the matter inexpensively, dispense with the need for a lengthy trial, and secure a monetary settlement. The plaintiffs and/or their attorney, however, demanded an excessive sum of money to resolve the matter. Interestingly, it was conceded that the surgery did not cause any real injury to the ear that was the subject of surgery and probably improved its condition. In fact, according to the defendant, the surgical ear also had a problem that likely would have required surgery in the near future. Our defense, therefore, was that damages were limited. Unable to convince the plaintiffs' lawyer that he and his clients were significantly overvaluing the case,

I realized that the matter would have to be tried. Although my client and I understood that a defense verdict was impossible, I also believed that the likelihood of a jury verdict in an amount that exceeded the settlement demand was slim. Indeed, the jury returned a verdict for the plaintiffs, but the monetary award was half of the settlement demand.

The date by which expert reports must be served will in most instances be dictated by the jurisdiction's applicable court rules and/or discovery orders entered by the court. Typically, the plaintiff's expert reports will be served within 60–90 days (approximately three months) after the completion of party depositions. Thereafter, your attorney will serve the reports of liability/causation/damages experts retained on your behalf.

Your liability expert will be a practitioner who practices in your field and who can identify the standard of care applicable to the treatment you provided and who can offer the opinion that you complied with the applicable standard of care. That same expert may be able to comment that your treatment did not cause or contribute to any injury claimed by the plaintiff and that the plaintiff's alleged damages were the result of a preexisting condition, the treatment of others, and/or the natural consequence of the plaintiff's underlying condition.

Your causation expert may not be someone who practices in your discipline but is competent to relate the plaintiff's claimed injuries to something other than the care that is criticized. A damages expert report will focus on the specific injuries allegedly sustained by the plaintiff and offer comments about the nature and substance of those claimed injuries and how they are unrelated to the treatment you provided.

Expert Depositions

In jurisdictions like New Jersey, depositions of malpractice experts are routinely conducted. In many respects, the deposition serves as a precursor to the expert's trial appearance and can provide both information and insight to the examining attorney. The deposition affords the opposing lawyer an opportunity to explore the expert's credentials and opinions. All attorneys involved in the matter are commonly present and entitled to conduct examination.

The expert deposition can be a relatively short or exceedingly protracted proceeding. The deposition's length depends on several factors, including the content of the expert's Curriculum Vitae, the number of defendants, the nature of the plaintiff's medical history, the complexity of the issues, the examining attorney's familiarity with the subject matter, the examining attorney's knowledge of the expert (as a result of the expert's participation in other matters), the length of the expert report, the number of opinions offered by the expert, the experience of the expert witness, and the style of the examining lawyer. Although a typical expert deposition may consume approximately three hours, there are exceptions.

Your attorney will use the deposition to gain both a better understanding of the plaintiff's expert and the expert's opinions. Defense counsel will seek to elicit testimony that may be valuable in several ways. Although the examination may appear "exploratory", your lawyer is probing for weaknesses or "soft spots" in the expert's opinions and will attempt to gain concessions from the plaintiff's expert. Experienced attorneys know that despite the conviction with which written opinions appear to be held, carefully crafted deposition questions may cause the adverse expert to reveal opinions favorable to your defense or to equivocate on certain pivotal issues.

All expert deposition transcripts likely will be furnished to you by your counsel with the stated expectation that you read those transcripts. It is never the intention of counsel to burden you with discovery materials to review. However, portions of the plaintiff's expert's testimony may reveal substantive opinions that warrant a discussion with your lawyer. Although defense counsel is experienced in medical malpractice matters, your insight and input will always be a welcome part of the defense effort.

Chapter 12

Settlement Option

The end point of any malpractice matter will be the jury trial unless the Complaint is dismissed for any number of procedural or substantive reasons during or at the end of the discovery period. Of course, an option to trial can be a monetary settlement. As you might appreciate, a trial is time-consuming and will impact your practice in a real and challenging way. A typical malpractice trial with you as the only defendant likely will consume at least two to three weeks, inclusive of jury selection, Opening Statements by counsel, the presentation of evidence, attorney Summations, the judge's Charge, jury deliberations, and the delivery of the verdict by the jury. If there are multiple defendants, the trial's length will be extended. If each party presents more than one expert, the trial will consume even more time. Additional non-expert lay witnesses will add to the trial's length. Of course, not every trial judge directs the movement of a trial at the same pace. Some judges move more quickly than others, and some interrupt the daily progression of a trial by presiding over other unrelated matters, like brief hearings or court conferences that might consume anywhere from 20 to 60 minutes each and which might delay the commencement time in the morning or cause the early

DOI: 10.4324/9781003459002-12

termination of the proceedings on a given day. Generally, a trial in most courts starts somewhere between 9 and 10 a.m. and ends between 4 and 5 p.m. Of course, there are brief 15-minute mid-morning and mid-afternoon breaks. A one-hour lunch break in the middle of the day is routine. It is expected, if not required that you be present in court with your attorney each day.

There may be days or portions of days when your lawyer is willing to excuse you from appearing for a compelling reason. But that will be a rarity. The concern is that your absence from court will be noticed by the jury and will not be well-received. After all, the plaintiff will be in court every day, conveying the clear message that the trial and its outcome are important enough to justify being present throughout. If the jurors are giving their time each day and willing to put their personal and professional lives on hold for the sake of assisting in the matter's resolution, they will think that you too should be present. You certainly do not want to disappoint the jurors in any way. Otherwise, you run the risk of offending the jury and sacrificing the outcome you seek.

Reasons to Consider Settlement

In the rare instance where you acknowledge having deviated from the accepted standard of care, settlement may be your only option and should be explored with defense counsel at your initial meeting. Even absent such concession, if an expert can not be found by your lawyer to support you despite multiple attempts, settlement will be discussed.

Settlement also may be considered for reasons unrelated to the merits of a case.

If you, your experts, and your counsel all agree that there was no departure from the standard of care in your treatment of the plaintiff, practical professional considerations nevertheless may prompt you to consider settling the matter before trial. For example, if you are a solo practitioner, you may need to close your office during the trial, which will impact patient care, your income, and the finances of your staff who may be out of work during your absence. In other words, business considerations may guide your thinking about proceeding to trial rather than the desire to seek vindication in court. Keep in mind, however, that just because you would prefer that the matter be settled, settlement might not always be achieved.

Of course, the upper limit of your insurance policy represents the most that your carrier is obligated to pay on your behalf. Frequently, a practitioner will have a $1,000,000/$3,000,000 policy. Some policies have limits of $3,000,000/$5,000,000. Of course, it is possible to obtain a policy with higher limits, although such a policy is infrequently offered or purchased. Your practice area and the likely damages that can result from improper care will impact the policy limits you select. Your insurance broker can provide guidance when securing a policy that best suits you and your circumstances. No matter the limits, the first figure represents the maximum amount that your carrier will pay for a single claim in a given policy year. The second figure is the total amount that your insurance company is obligated to pay in satisfaction of multiple claims in a policy year.

Unprotected Conduct

You should understand that your insurance policy will cover acts of negligence, that is, conduct that allegedly constitutes deviations from the standard of care. It will not and cannot under the law cover intentional or deliberate acts of misconduct or fraudulent behavior. Nor will it provide coverage for contract violations, if any. At times, the Complaint will include some or all of the non-covered claims, though there may not be a true or developed factual basis for such claims. If that is the case, at the appropriate time during discovery, your attorney will consider filing a motion to dismiss such baseless claims. It can be expected that before that happens, your interests will be defended in their entirety. Piecemeal representation is not ideal and likely will not happen.

If your counsel is unsuccessful in obtaining dismissal of the non-negligence claims, your lawyer will recommend that you retain personal counsel to defend such claims. It is expected that personal counsel also will address the issue of protecting your assets to the extent necessary or possible.

In a routine malpractice matter, the Complaint will seek compensatory monetary damages which are intended to compensate the plaintiff for the alleged injuries. On occasion, a plaintiff will include a claim for punitive damages, which are designed to punish a defendant for acts that are willful, malicious, or wanton, or which are in utter disregard for the safety, health, or well-being of the plaintiff. There are few suits that legitimately support such damages. At times, a plaintiff's attorney will seek such damages because it is believed, albeit mistakenly, that doing so serves to strengthen the claims and may prompt the defendant to settle the matter earlier rather than later. As with the dismissal of non-negligence claims, your attorney will seek dismissal of meritless punitive damage claims at the proper time during discovery. Like non-negligence claims, punitive damages are not covered by your malpractice policy, as they are based on alleged intentional behavior.

Consequently, your personal assets will be exposed and arguably available to satisfy a punitive damages jury verdict and resultant judgment. If your lawyer is unable to obtain dismissal of the plaintiff's punitive damages claims, you will need to retain personal counsel to provide guidance.

No matter the reason for retention of personal counsel, you should seek the services of an attorney who has medical malpractice experience. If you do not know such a lawyer, your malpractice attorney likely will be able to make a recommendation. The degree to which personal counsel will get involved in the day-to-day handling of the matter depends on what you and personal counsel agree needs to be done moving forward. You must keep in mind that your malpractice attorney will handle all aspects of discovery and, notwithstanding the involvement of personal counsel, will fully defend you through discovery. Expect that your malpractice counsel and your personal attorney will confer about the division of responsibility.

You should understand that your insurance policy likely contains a cooperation clause, which means that notwithstanding your preference for settlement, your insurance company, guided in part by your counsel's assessment of the case, may not want to settle the matter. Should that happen, you must cooperate with your lawyer in the matter's preparation for trial. You also will be expected to appear in court each trial day.

Should you advise your lawyer that you would like to see the case settled, and your policy contains a consent provision, you will be instructed to execute your carrier's standard Consent to Settle form. But an executed Consent to Settle form will not guarantee settlement. If the plaintiff's counsel demands a sum that far exceeds the case's reasonable settlement value and your lawyer is unable to negotiate that figure down to an acceptable range, settlement likely will not happen, and you can expect a trial.

It is not unusual for a plaintiff's attorney to send a letter to your lawyer demanding that the carrier engage in meaningful settlement discussions when the plaintiff's attorney's perceived value of the matter exceeds the policy limit. In New Jersey, such correspondence is called a *Rova Farms* letter, based on the *Rova Farms* court decision, which stands for the proposition that an insurance company has a fiduciary obligation to engage in good faith settlement discussions where the factual circumstances of the case dictate and where the potential exists for a jury verdict that will exceed the defendant's policy limit. In such a situation, your lawyer will advise you to retain personal counsel in much the same way as noted above. Your personal attorney, among other things, will then send a letter to your retained counsel and/or your insurance company requesting that the case be settled within your policy limits, which by definition requires you to sign a Consent to Settle form. Keep in mind that under the law, your insurance company is not obligated to settle your case in response to a *Rova Farms* letter. Its obligation is to act reasonably under the circumstances of your matter in conducting settlement discussions through your attorney. Those discussions may prove beneficial in securing a settlement, or they may be fruitless. Again, the law only requires reasonable behavior by your insurance company, not a settlement guarantee.

In fact, there are various reasons why a case might not be settled. The facts may not warrant settlement and may justify aggressively defending the plaintiff's claims through trial. It may be that a reasonable settlement offer has been rejected by the plaintiff. Perhaps the settlement demand is so excessive that a responding offer cannot and frankly should not be made. It may be that good faith negotiations have progressed to a point of impasse and neither party is willing to move from the last figure demanded or offered. No matter the reason, without a settlement, the likely endpoint of a suit is trial.

Of course, as the trial unfolds, adverse events may prompt the plaintiff's attorney to reconsider and reduce a previous settlement demand. Perhaps a witness testified in an unexpected manner or a motion by defense counsel eliminated certain liability claims or reduced some of the monetary damage claims. Alternatively, trial developments that negatively impact the defense of your case might also warrant a reconsideration of your attorney or insurance carrier's settlement posture and can prompt an increase in a pre-trial settlement offer.

Importantly, a case can be settled at any point during the trial or even as late as the end of the trial after Summations. So, even after the trial commences, settlement remains a possibility if circumstances warrant. Understand that your attorney is constantly assessing the impact of trial evidence and judicial rulings on the progression of the case. It is not unusual for counsel to provide daily trial reports to your insurance company representative, and if trial events require reassessment of the defense's pre-trial settlement posture, your carrier might be willing to increase the settlement authority given to your lawyer so that settlement discussions can resume. Perhaps with the active assistance of the trial judge, a settlement can be negotiated, and the matter concluded. Of course, if your policy contains a consent provision, as frequently occurs, your written consent will be needed before meaningful settlement discussions can occur and certainly before a settlement can be achieved.

Mediation

Settlement assistance also may be provided at any time during the pendency of a matter by a mediator. Although some attorneys provide effective mediation services, an increasing number of retired trial judges are becoming rather capable mediators. The ability to bring the parties together in mediation and effectively assist in the resolution of a case are skills that are rare but greatly appreciated. Mediators are selected by the agreement of all counsel, and many have proven to be capable and effective, making them attractive to both the plaintiff's and the defense bar.

Mediation is an informal process that does not take place in a courtroom. Witnesses do not appear, and no testimony of any kind is offered. Routinely, mediation is conducted at the mediator's office. The mediator will ask each lawyer to submit to the mediator a confidential Mediation Statement well in advance of the mediation, which will not be furnished to other counsel. The Statement will identify the relevant facts and legal issues. It will recite the strength of the party's case and the weaknesses of the adverse party's position. Documents obtained during discovery that support a party's factual and/or legal position are routinely attached to the Statement, along with a detailed analysis of those documents. Such items may include a party's interrogatory answers, excerpts from a party's deposition, expert reports and/or excerpts from expert depositions. Ultimately, a party's Mediation Statement will contain argument intended to persuade the mediator of that party's position, the likelihood of a favorable jury verdict should the matter proceed to trial, as well as the financial value of the case. It is expected that the mediator will review the parties' Mediation Statements and attached discovery documents in advance of the mediation session so as to become fully familiar with the pertinent facts and issues.

Mediation may begin with a brief initial meeting in the mediator's conference room where the plaintiff's attorney, defense counsel, and the plaintiff have assembled. The insurance company representative also may be a participant. The mediator will provide an introduction, and the mediator's prior career milestones will be highlighted. The mediator will then discuss the way mediation will proceed and invite the different sides to move to separate smaller conference rooms or offices. The plaintiff with counsel will move to one room, and your counsel will move to another. Your insurance carrier representative usually is required to be present (or be available by phone or via Zoom in the alternative), simply because settlement discussions might only prove fruitful if actual offers can be communicated through the representative at the mediation. The plaintiff is expected to appear with the plaintiff's attorney so that decisions can be made in response to any offer made.

The mediator is expected to move from room to room to speak confidentially with the different sides. Having received information from one side, the mediator will then speak confidentially with the adverse contingent and exchange pertinent information to bring the parties closer to a settlement. In defense counsel's presence, the mediator may speak directly to the insurance carrier representative about the amount of money the representative has to resolve a matter. The mediator will discuss the strengths and weaknesses of the case with the defense attorney to determine the reasonableness of the defense's valuation of the matter and to ascertain the maximum amount the defense may be willing to offer in settlement. Of course, the mediator is expected to determine the case's value. In the presence of the plaintiff's counsel, the mediator may speak directly to the plaintiff about the amount that might be considered in full resolution of the matter. The mediator likely will identify the strengths and weaknesses of the plaintiff's case.

The complexity of the case, the number of parties, and the mediator's ability to secure concessions from all counsel largely dictate the mediation's length. It is not unusual for mediation to last a whole day or even consume multiple sessions. If mediation requires more than one session, mediators may opt against scheduling successive mediation dates. Breaks in the mediation schedule might prove helpful by giving the participants a chance to consider and reconsider their settlement positions.

Settlement Impact

Understandably, a defendant may be concerned about a settlement's impact on professional reputation, insurance premiums, and available future insurance coverage. Those same concerns may arise when a matter is tried and a verdict for a plaintiff is returned by a jury. Although reasonable concerns, the priority should always be a favorable and realistic resolution of the matter at hand, if possible. Insurance coverage and insurance premium issues should be secondary concerns. As a practical matter, carriers have an internal formula that is used when determining whether an insured's policy will be renewed, or the degree to which future premiums will be increased. Since a defendant has no control over these issues or how they are handled by an insurance company, it is best to not give them much consideration when contemplating the settlement of a case.

It also is recommended that a defendant not be distracted by the reporting of a settled case to the National Practitioner's Data Bank and/or local licensing boards. Such reporting should not dissuade a defendant from considering settlement when it is advisable to do so.

Some practitioners will consider settling a matter with personal funds rather than having the insurance company make the payment. Also, if an adverse trial verdict is returned, a defendant may pay the verdict amount from personal assets. Of course, this only happens when the settlement or verdict amount is one that the practitioner can afford to pay. The National Practitioner's Data Bank does not require the reporting of settlements or verdicts if the payment is made by the individual defendant and not the insurance carrier. Though it may vary from state to state, a defendant is not required to report to a local licensing board a settlement payment or verdict payment from personal funds as opposed to carrier funds. A discussion with your counsel about these issues is suggested.

If an insurance company does not pay a settlement or verdict from carrier funds, it is reasonable to conclude that the occurrence of a settlement or adverse verdict will not significantly impact policy renewal or future premium amounts. Again, you can seek confirmation from your attorney.

Chapter 13

Trial Preparation

Individual Effort

As your lawyer prepares for trial, so should you. Your attorney will receive notification from the court when a trial date is assigned well in advance of the actual date. If discovery has been completed and all attorneys, parties, and witnesses are available on the assigned date, the potential exists that the matter will be assigned to a specific judge for trial. Importantly, the assignment of an initial trial date by the court does not necessarily mean that the trial will commence as scheduled even if all discovery has been completed and all anticipated trial participants are available. No matter the jurisdiction, frequently there are more cases ready for trial on a given court date than there are available trial judges. The shortage of judges greatly impacts how quickly or slowly, cases are tried. And it is for this reason that matters that are trial-ready do not necessarily start trial on the assigned date.

So, when your lawyer alerts you to a trial date, you need to ask whether the date is realistic. It is possible that you will receive notifications of various trial dates before your counsel advises that a particular date is real. Once a realistic date is

 DOI: 10.4324/9781003459002-13

scheduled, there are certain matters that you must address. These issues involve the cancellation of patient visits and/or the necessity of closing your office.

If you are a sole practitioner, rescheduling patient appointments will be part of the preparation process. If there is little for your staff to do without you and patients in the office, you may have to temporarily close the office. If members of your staff have responsibilities that will keep them busy in your absence, then closing may be unnecessary. Of course, seek guidance from your lawyer as to whether trial will commence on the court-assigned date. It would be unfortunate if you were to cancel patients in anticipation of a trial and then later learn that the date is uncertain or that the court has adjourned the trial for any number of reasons.

Obviously, time in court is time away from your practice, and although it is not an ideal situation for your practice, your presence in court throughout the trial is essential. The trial witness schedule typically cannot be determined with certainty until the attorneys initially confer with the trial judge. Your lawyer will share the witness schedule with you and discuss when your testimony will be needed. Even then, as the trial progresses, last-minute changes to the trial schedule for any number of reasons can and likely will occur. You certainly can ask your attorney whether there are any days or partial days when you might be excused from appearing in court. Keep in mind that such absences should be kept to a minimum, as the jury likely will not react well to your nonappearance, especially since the individual jurors are not given time off during the trial to attend to personal matters. Each juror must be present during each moment of the trial, regardless of the importance of a witness testifying on a given day. However, if there is a day or partial day when you absolutely cannot appear in court, your counsel may be willing to grant permission for a limited absence. In a civil trial, it is not required by law or court rule that you be present throughout.

However, it is in your best interest to be a daily participant. Keep in mind that the plaintiff will absolutely be in court each trial day to demonstrate obvious dedication to the outcome. You should demonstrate that same degree of interest by your daily presence. Otherwise, the jury may believe, albeit mistakenly, that you don't really care about the trial or its outcome. The jurors will be giving of themselves, having placed their personal and/or work lives on hold to assist in the resolution of your case. They will not readily accept what appears to be a lack of commitment by you to the process.

Meeting With Counsel

Prior to the commencement of the trial, your counsel will schedule at least one pre-trial conference with you. The purpose is to prepare you to testify. In my opinion, it is best for the conference to be divided into multiple meetings, the first of which will occur approximately two weeks prior to the trial. During this meeting, your lawyer will discuss what is expected to occur at the trial. Events, like pre-trial motions submitted by your attorney or opposing counsel, which may substantively impact the trial, or the anticipated testimony of witnesses will be discussed. A motion is best described as a written application submitted by a lawyer which seeks some type of relief before the trial begins. In response to a motion, adverse counsel will submit written opposition.

Expect your attorney to describe how the trial will proceed in some detail. You will be advised about the type of introductory remarks to be made by the trial judge at the outset, Jury Selection, Opening Statements, the sequence of witness testimony and documents counsel expects to use as evidence, Summations, the Jury Charge, deliberations and the reporting of a verdict. The Court's Charge to the jury is a shorthand way to describe that part of the trial where the trial judge reads the applicable law of that state to the jurors, which is needed before a verdict can be rendered. Your attorney will explain that the judge will instruct the jury that it must accept the law as stated and then apply that law to the facts as determined by the jury.

Counsel will tell you that the judge will require a reasoned and dispassionate consideration of the evidence presented during the trial. As you might expect, the jury will then retire to the jury room with the physical evidence admitted during the trial, and its members will exchange views and thoughts about the evidence. Once a verdict has been reached, the jury will reassemble in the courtroom and deliver the verdict before the judge and all the parties and counsel.

You will be told where all the trial participants will be seated, inclusive of the jurors, as well as the usual dynamic among all the trial participants. Your attorney will describe how you should dress for the trial and the degree to which you can interact with your counsel in the courtroom in the presence of the jury. Expect to receive guidance on how to prepare for your testimony. At a minimum, counsel will instruct you as to the documents you should read in advance of the trial and in preparation for your testimony. In most instances, that preparation will include reviewing the pertinent chart entries, your interrogatory answers, your deposition, the plaintiff's deposition, the plaintiff's expert reports that support the plaintiff's claims against you, and the reports of experts retained on your behalf. You may also be asked to read the depositions of the plaintiff's experts and those of your experts.

Although you may have reviewed these documents when initially supplied by your counsel, reading them again is essential to reacquaint yourself with the documents' details. Once you have completed your assignment, your lawyer likely will want to meet with you to discuss the items reviewed. You can be assured that your counsel will have reviewed the very same documents in preparation for the trial and will be able to discuss their contents with you. Thereafter, a third meeting likely will be scheduled, the purpose of which will be to prepare for direct examination by your attorney and the anticipated cross-examination by adverse counsel.

There are multiple ways to answer any question, and your lawyer will guide you as to the best way to respond to questions asked at trial. Of course, you never want to provide courtroom testimony that is inconsistent with your responses to interrogatory answers or deposition testimony. If, upon reading your interrogatory responses and/or deposition, you determine that you cannot legitimately offer the same information in court for any reason, or that the discovery supplied is inconsistent with the facts as you understand them, you must alert your counsel. A minor, benign, or innocent misstatement in discovery can be addressed in court if your attorney deems it necessary. More serious inaccuracies or factual errors will need to be discussed with your lawyer, and a strategy established for the most effective way of dealing with the inconsistencies.

You may think to raise the issue of settlement as an option to trial with your attorney during one of the pre-trial sessions. It is not unusual for you to be concerned about the impact a trial will have on the day-to-day operation of your practice, and for that reason and perhaps for that reason only, you might express an interest in settlement. Although your defense may have been well-prepared and both you and your lawyer are confident that a formidable defense can be presented to a jury, you may still be reluctant to commit to a time-consuming trial. Keep in mind, however, that your insurance carrier will not agree to authorize your lawyer to negotiate a settlement just because you would prefer seeing patients to seeing a jury. Unfortunately, that factor alone will not motivate an insurance company to initiate settlement discussions.

Trial preparation may prompt your lawyer to seek the assistance of a witness consultant. Your counsel will want you to be the best trial witness possible, and if achieving that goal requires such help, expect to devote some time to meeting with a witness consultant who will provide additional guidance as to how to conduct yourself on the witness stand and how to present yourself in a way that makes you an appealing trial witness. Maximizing witness effectiveness will be the consultant's goal, and implementing approaches to optimize favorable testimony will be introduced at the meeting with the consultant. Conferences with a witness consultant may not involve your counsel and may last as long as six hours. It likely will be a one-on-one exchange with the consultant. Although your lawyer will review expected questioning by the plaintiff's attorney at trial, the witness consultant will also engage in this exercise. The mock questions that the witness consultant will ask are typically more generic in nature than specific to the facts of the case. But the words used in your answers will be analyzed, and better ways to respond and convey the same information will be explored.

Defense counsel, your witness consultant if needed, and you will share the responsibility of working toward the goal of molding you into a witness whose testimony the jury will find reasonable, if not compelling. It is essential that the jury be willing to embrace you and your defense.

Chapter 14

The Trial

Other than when a case settles or is dismissed, everything culminates in the trial. A successful trial outcome requires that each phase of the trial be carefully executed. One phase involves the presentation of defense witnesses, not the least important of whom is you. If you have reviewed the documents your attorney has asked you to read, participated in pre-trial meetings with your lawyer as directed, and cleared your professional calendar and mind so as to focus only on what is about to unfold, you should be ready for the process.

Your Environment

There is no doubt that the courtroom will be foreign territory to you. As a tangible symbol of the law, the courtroom's trappings are largely based on tradition and are reflective of a palpable melding of custom and purpose. Your effectiveness as a trial witness requires that you understand the environment in which you will be expected to perform. You must be comfortable in the courtroom, and you must appear comfortable to the jury. A defendant who seems ill at ease on the witness stand will be poorly received by jurors. Even the most

 DOI: 10.4324/9781003459002-14

solid practitioner will seem less credible and less persuasive if unable to comfortably function in court.

In order to achieve some degree of comfort, you must understand the physical environment and the roles of the typical trial participants. Since you likely spend most of your time in a hospital or practice office where your comfort level is high, the courtroom will present a new challenge. Even if you do a fair amount of public speaking at conferences and lectures, you still will be out of your element in court.

Since you will be expected to sit in court with your counsel from the trial's inception, you likely will become more at ease with your new environment with each passing day. Before the presentation of witnesses, the process of jury selection and the attorneys' Opening Statements will consume enough time to allow you to understand and appreciate your surroundings. Being comfortable in the courtroom should equate with a level of comfort on the witness stand once you're called as a witness. As you watch the proceedings, you will learn the behavioral tendencies of the various "players" in the trial. Appreciate the dynamics of the relationship between and among the components of the trial – the judge (sometimes referred to as "the court"), the jury, the plaintiff's attorney, your attorney, the plaintiff, you, the court officer (or bailiff), the court clerk, and occasionally the judge's law clerk. Watch the jurors and their reaction to trial events – attorney questions, witness answers, objections by counsel, the judge's rulings, physical movement by attorneys and witnesses, and the use of trial aids and exhibits. You will be amazed at how your anxiety level will decrease.

Trial Sequence

In addition to appreciating the physical characteristics of the courtroom and the role of each participant, you should understand how a trial proceeds and some of the more general "rules" of behavior in court.

The trial begins with a brief statement by the judge to the prospective jurors about the nature of the case, the allegations, and the defenses. The jurors are randomly selected from hundreds of county residents summoned to the courthouse by legal notice that day to potentially serve as trial jurors. In most jurisdictions, judges who need jurors to serve on a trial jury will have their court clerk contact the jury assembly manager, who will then designate a number of individuals in the jury assembly room for that trial. The group of jurors routinely is referred to as a jury panel. That panel, which likely will be comprised of between 30 and 50 individuals, is accompanied by a court officer to the judge's courtroom. Once the group of selected jurors reaches the courtroom, they are seated in the rows behind counsel table, and the jury selection process begins.

The judge will enter the courtroom and be introduced by the court officer. In some courtrooms, such introduction is handled by the judge. The judge will then introduce the attorneys. Each lawyer will introduce his or her client and identify the party's anticipated trial witnesses. The prospective jurors provide information about themselves in open court in response to questions posed by the judge and/or counsel. The trial judge will excuse certain individuals from service "for cause", that is, due to personal experiences, familiarity with the parties, attorneys or witnesses, financial hardship, medical reasons, language difficulties, a pre-arranged vacation, work requirements, or personal/family obligations. The court can excuse an infinite number of jurors "for cause". Each of the attorneys may excuse from service certain of the jurors, as well. Generally, an attorney can exercise a "peremptory" challenge and excuse a prospective juror for an undisclosed reason consistent with prevailing law without articulating the reason. However, the presumption is that the juror has identified something in his or her background or has displayed a characteristic that the attorney believes might reasonably suggest a bias either against his client or in favor of the adverse party. Absent exceptional circumstances, each lawyer is given a fixed number of peremptory jury challenges. Once those challenges are exhausted, counsel cannot seek to eliminate any further prospective jurors without cause.

Typically, after jury selection and preliminary remarks or instructions by the trial judge, the substantive trial begins with an Opening Statement by the plaintiff's attorney (whose seat at counsel table is closest to the jury box), followed by the Opening Statement of your lawyer (whose seat at counsel table is furthest from the jury box). If the trial involves multiple defendants, the sequence of defense Opening Statements will follow the order in which the various defendants have been named in the Complaint. Witnesses and evidence will then be presented by the plaintiff's attorney, at the conclusion of which, the plaintiff will "rest". The defense case is then presented with witnesses and other evidence. Again, if there are multiple defendants, each defendant presents his or her case in the same order as Opening Statements. Each defendant will "rest" at the conclusion of that defendant's presentation of witnesses and evidence. In rare instances, the plaintiff may present "rebuttal" evidence in response to unanticipated critical evidence offered by the defense.

After the presentation of all evidence, a Summation or Closing Argument will be offered by each attorney. The sequence will be the opposite of the Opening Statements. Opening and closing remarks by the lawyers are not evidence, and the jury is so advised by the trial judge. The court then instructs the jurors as to the law that applies to the case, called the "Jury Charge". The jury is obligated during deliberations to apply the law recited by the trial judge to the facts as it finds existed based on the evidence. Following deliberations in the jury room (which may take minutes or days), the jury records its decision on a Jury Verdict Sheet and then returns to the courtroom to verbally announce its verdict in open court to the judge, the parties, and their counsel. The Jury Verdict Sheet will be discussed in detail in a later section.

Trial Events

During trial, counsel will often address the court using rather formal language intended to convey a sense of respect properly due the trial judge. It is expected that counsel also will be addressed by the court with appropriate respect. Witnesses also are to be treated with respect by examining counsel. And of course, the jury is deserving of the respect of all trial participants.

When it is necessary, address the trial judge as "Your Honor". Although you may invoke the more casual term "Judge", use it less frequently than "Your Honor". Refer to your attorney and adverse counsel as "Mr _____", "Ms _____", or "Counsel". Unless instructed otherwise by your lawyer, parties should be referred to as "Mr _____", "Ms _____", or "Dr _____".

The trial judge may interrupt your response to a question at any time during your testimony. If this should happen, stop talking and defer to the court and its need to comment. If your testimony is interrupted by a remark from counsel (typically an objection), stop and allow the attorney to complete his or her statement and await instructions from the court or the examining lawyer as to whether or how you may proceed.

A typical and repeated occurrence during a trial is the sidebar conference. Over time, it serves as a source of annoyance and frustration to witnesses and jurors alike. A "sidebar" conference is a mini meeting between the trial judge and counsel. It takes place alongside the judge's bench on the side opposite the witness stand and may be convened at the direction of the trial judge or at the request of one of the attorneys. The remarks by the trial judge and counsel are not intended for witness or jury consumption. Consequently, voices are in low tones so as to minimize the possibility that a witness or a juror may overhear the discussion. A sidebar often occurs in response to an objection by one of the lawyers to a question or as a result of testimony elicited from a witness. In such an instance, the topic of discussion is one that involves issues of law and/or evidence. Procedural or scheduling matters may also be addressed at sidebar.

Although exceptions exist, most sidebars are brief, usually lasting from 30 seconds to 5 minutes. If, after the sidebar begins, it appears to the trial judge that the conference will consume significantly more time, the court may direct the jury to return to the jury room, and the witness may be asked by the judge to temporarily leave the courtroom. Excusing the jurors and the witness protects them from overhearing the sidebar. Possibly prejudicial comments by counsel, which jurors and perhaps witnesses overhear, may be the basis for a mistrial and the subsequent need to start the trial process anew at a later date with a new jury.

At the conclusion of the sidebar, the trial judge will typically advise the jury as to the court's ruling in response to the objection of counsel or otherwise remark to the extent necessary. If the ruling impacts you as the trial witness, an instruction from the court will be offered. In such instance, comply with the judge's direction and, if appropriate, respectfully acknowledge the judge's comments with a simple "Yes, Your Honor" or similar response.

Of course, multiple sidebar conferences during your testimony can be disruptive and render your testimony less effective. In fact, sidebars necessitated by the plaintiff's attorney's constant objections may be part of a deliberate effort to rattle you. No matter how frustrating, don't let the interruptions "throw you". Maintain your composure and, when permitted by the trial judge to continue, do so smoothly. Focus on the substance of your testimony and ignore adverse counsel's maneuvers.

Also potentially problematic is the "dead time" created by the sidebar. While the sidebar conference takes place, you may be on the witness stand in front of the jury. Members of the jury likely are watching you, trying to "size you up". Don't squirm in your seat, tug at your collar, or nervously shuffle the papers in front of you. Although you may not talk to the jury, the interlude presents an opportunity to enhance your rapport with the jury. Instead of looking away from the jury, you may make brief eye contact with the jurors. Look their way in a relaxed, easy, and confident fashion.

Also, be aware that the judge may question you during your testimony. Such questioning typically is infrequent, and there is no way to predict whether or when it will occur. Customarily, the court poses queries when the judge feels that those asked by the attorneys do not fully explore a significant issue. A judge may also question a witness where the testimony is confusing, meandering, or evasive (unintentionally or deliberately). Although many judges are reluctant to assume the role of lawyer, it is the court's duty to ensure that the evidence is fairly and completely presented to the jury. To that end, therefore, judges at times inject themselves into the examination process in order to assist the jury in its fact-finding effort. Accordingly, you must be prepared to field court-initiated questions, which are typically direct and pointed. Needless to say, answer them forthrightly. Judges have far less tolerance than do attorneys for answers that are circuitous or confusing. Even if the judge appears to incorporate the position of the plaintiff in the questions posed or to adopt an adversarial tone, respond with the requisite respect and avoid being combative.

Finally, the trial judge may permit jurors to question witnesses after the attorneys complete their examination. Typically, jury questions are handwritten by jurors and then reviewed by the trial judge and counsel. They may be slightly modified by the judge where appropriate and then presented verbally to the witness by the judge. Respond with the same care as you would in answering questions posed by your lawyer, the plaintiff's attorney, or the trial judge.

Understanding Your Role

As the defendant, your trial testimony will be key. Keep in mind that the courtroom is the domain of the trial judge. Your presentation will be limited by the rules known by your attorney and the plaintiff's counsel and enforced by the judge. It is not your prerogative to control any aspect of the trial other than your testimony. Accept direction from your lawyer and respond to instructions offered by the trial judge.

The trial is fluid. The expected date and time of your testimony at the outset typically are based on how quickly or slowly the trial progresses. Witness scheduling at the outset often is revised as the trial unfolds. Scheduling is affected by numerous factors over which your attorney may have little or no control, such as (1) the length of jury selection; (2) obligations of the judge that disrupt the trial; (3) the length of witness testimony; (4) court recesses; (5) unanticipated protracted legal arguments; (6) the frequency and duration of sidebar conferences; and (7) miscellaneous "down time". Also, infrequently, an unanticipated trial development prompts a change in trial strategy, and the plaintiff's attorney or your counsel may determine that a scheduled witness may not be needed, that a witness the plaintiff's lawyer or your counsel initially did not plan to call becomes necessary, or that the anticipated order in which witnesses were to be presented must change.

As a defense attorney, my client typically is my first trial witness. It is through the defendant's testimony that the jury will learn what I consider to be the essential facts of the case. You are the "table setter" in a manner of speaking. After testifying about your credentials and the nature of your practice, you will provide the jury with the underlying story of your involvement in the plaintiff's care. Notwithstanding the information supplied by the plaintiff and the plaintiff's witnesses, the jury will be anxious to hear from you and your recitation of the facts. The jury will want you to explain the circumstances surrounding your reasoning for decisions made, treatment recommended, and procedures performed. If you are able to satisfy the jury's thirst for clear and cogent explanations for all that you thought and did, the jurors may become allies rather than enemies in the quest for a defense verdict.

Keep in mind that providing reasonable testimony in response to questions posed by your counsel isn't even half the battle. The true test that you will confront and must pass in order to be a successful witness depends on the testimony you give in response to the plaintiff's attorney's questions.

Courtroom Demeanor

Knowing that the jurors will be anxiously awaiting your testimony, capture their interest from the start by providing direct, articulate, and confident responses to questions posed. Typically, jurors will listen with a relatively open mind, and if you grab their attention with the logic of your thoughts and the certainty of your testimony, that elusive yet essential goal of jury acceptance may be yours.

In essence, the way in which you comport yourself will be a key to success on the witness stand. Certain of the intangibles that comprise demeanor are worth reviewing.

Confidence is critical and cannot be underestimated. However, there is a fine line between confidence and arrogance. Given lay tendencies to view physicians in the real world as arrogant, it is not surprising that jurors might perceive you with a jaundiced eye. Consequently, when testifying, do so with confidence but always guard against tripping over the line that divides confidence and arrogance.

The jurors need to see you as a confident individual. In my view, a confident witness is one who testifies with energy and conviction. Always focus on the attorney questioning you, whether it is your lawyer or the lawyer representing the plaintiff. By that, I mean, look at the attorney as questions are asked. Let it be clear to the jury that you are intent on listening to the question and equally clear that you are eager to respond. Of course, while waiting for a question to be asked, you should appear poised, not weak or ineffectual. Do not fidget in your seat or look at the ceiling or glance at the floor. The jury's perception of you as a confident witness may result in part from your actions even when you are not actually speaking. Given the fact that the jury will be watching you throughout your time on the witness stand, never do anything that will be ill-received. Do not avoid eye contact with the jurors. In fact, you should embrace the opportunity to look at the jury both while waiting for a question and while testifying. Do your best to not appear nervous or anxious.

Always keep your emotions in check, especially during questioning by adverse counsel. Never allow your "buttons to be pushed". The importance of remaining calm and collected during all of your testimony cannot be overemphasized. Do not appear angry, aggravated, or disgusted. Although the trial process is imposing, it is imperative that you not allow the jury to sense any of those emotions in you.

I can tell you from experience that a trial that has gone well up to the point of the defendant's testimony can be completely upended by that defendant's poor performance on the witness stand. You will be counseled by your attorney during pre-trial meetings as to how to comport yourself on the witness stand. Do not allow countless hours of prep time by you and your lawyer to go unrewarded by a momentary or series of momentary lapses in behavior on the witness stand because you were unable to keep your composure.

You may perceive certain tactics by the plaintiff's attorney to constitute needling or badgering. You might consider the lawyer to be somewhat unpleasant, abrasive, or cantankerous. You might characterize the plaintiff's lawyer's questions as unfair or unreasonable. You may be offended by the fact that you have been forced to explain yourself or that you have been forced to go through the litigation process in the first place. Reasons to dislike the plaintiff's counsel or the questions posed are endless. But under no circumstance should your innermost negative thoughts about the plaintiff's lawyer or, for that matter, the plaintiff, come to the surface.

During questioning by adverse counsel, do your best to avoid looking at your attorney for extended periods. It's not unusual for a defendant to occasionally glance in the direction of defense counsel while testifying to seek comfort. The desire to look at your lawyer may be prompted by a need for reassurance or support from counsel. That sign likely will never come, even if your performance is compelling. You will not see a thumbs-up, a head nod, or a smile.

You certainly won't see any reaction from your lawyer if you're doing poorly. Your attorney knows better than to display emotion, no matter what is happening during the trial. In sum, frequent and/or extended looks at your counsel should be avoided because the jury may think you are tentative or uncertain. A reaction you absolutely do not want. The damage that a faltering demeanor may cause may not be readily cured.

Be reminded that your testimony is delivered from the witness stand in a seated position. If you're accustomed to speaking in more open forums like medical conferences or seminars, the restraints imposed by the confines of the courtroom may prove uncomfortable or unsettling. I've seen a witness repeatedly tilt the chair back on its rear legs (tempting fate in the process), and I have seen a witness unknowingly rock back and forth in the chair on the witness stand while testifying. Both appeared uneasy, and their behavior, at the least, detracted from their testimony. Avoid behavior which is distracting to the jury or which may appear to manifest anxiety.

If you have experience as a lecturer, you might be more comfortable standing in front of the jury when testifying. Mention this to your attorney while preparing for trial and jointly identify those portions of your testimony that might be more effective if delivered from a standing position. Of course, you can only do so with the trial judge's permission and only for good reason. Candidly, a judge rarely will deny counsel's request for permission to have a witness testify from a standing position. If your testimony requires the use of trial exhibits, the court likely will allow you to stand in front of the jury box. Enlargements of patient records, anatomical drawings, models, and computer-based presentations are often used at trial. Their use in conjunction with your testimony can serve as a valid reason for you to leave the witness stand. The result may well be a less staid presentation and a more relaxed performance.

No matter the location from which you testify, always remember to connect with each juror on an individual basis. This topic will be addressed below in significant detail. It bears mentioning, however, that you should consider your audience and, given its rather small size, speak to and look into the eyes of each jury member at least once during the course of your testimony. Forge an alliance with the jurors on a person-to-person basis and look for a physical reaction from each individual with whom you have connected. A subtle smile or head nod may be an encouraging sign.

Question Responsiveness

Answering questions at trial in a direct fashion suggests forth-rightness and enhances credibility. With proper preparation, this should be handily accomplished when responding to planned examination by your lawyer. Questioning by adverse counsel likely will present more of a challenge. If you have devoted sufficient time to testimony preparation, however, you should fare reasonably well. No matter who is question-ing you, always remember to respond with an answer that is reasonably responsive to the question posed. Do not meander, evade, or deflect. Focus on the question and provide a mean-ingful answer without volunteering extraneous or collateral information, especially when being questioned by adverse counsel. If you provide an answer that clearly is not respon-sive to the question asked, adverse counsel will ask that you refocus on the question just posed rather than answering a question not asked. If you repeatedly fail to answer counsel's questions, the plaintiff's lawyer likely will request that the trial judge direct you to answer the pending question. Counsel may also ask the judge to strike your answer as not responsive and instruct the jury to disregard it. The court may admonish you to listen to the question and answer what's being asked. Should it get to the point where it looks to the jury that you are difficult and unwilling to directly answer questions, you may be unable to fully recover from the jury's perception that you are evasive and not worthy of belief. Never let that happen.

It bears mentioning that adverse counsel may direct you to respond to certain questions with a simple "yes" or "no" answer. However, if you are unable to respond in that fashion, you cannot be forced to do so despite such instruction.

Jurors in the courtroom, like people you encounter every day in the real world, admire candor. Evasiveness is not a quality to which individuals favorably respond. If you attempt to answer questions in a direct fashion and do so repeatedly, you will gain the jury's respect. This is a most important step in achieving the type of rapport that will place you in a position of advantage.

More importantly, to the extent that juries equate candor with honesty, the significance of question responsiveness cannot be underestimated. An evasive witness (or at least one who appears evasive) will be squarely rejected by the jury. Should that occur, ultimate trial success may be out of reach. If you impress the jury as honest, however, the battle to gain juror acceptance likely will be won, as might be the trial itself.

Thus, the cumulative effect of multiple non-responsive answers can be devastating. Since your testimony is central to a successful trial, rejection by the jury for such conduct likely will derail that outcome. Remember, if a subject is sufficiently significant, your lawyer will always have an opportunity on redirect examination to go back to those matters addressed by adverse counsel in an effort to have you more fully explain testimony deliberately restricted by cross-examination. Do not risk damage to yourself by trying to circumvent the limitations intentionally imposed by the plaintiff's attorney. Such effort will create more problems than it will solve.

The length of direct examination will be governed by various factors including but not necessarily limited to: (1) the frequency of your contacts with the plaintiff; (2) the nature and length of treatment provided to the plaintiff; (3) whether treatment was rendered in an office and/or hospital setting; (4) the type and frequency of contact with other providers involved in the plaintiff's care; (5) the complexity of the plaintiff's condition; and (6) the complexity of the treatment rendered. Direct examination typically lasts between 60 minutes and 3 hours.

After direct examination is concluded, adverse counsel will conduct cross-examination, the length of which is variable. It might be as short as 30 minutes or as long as 2 hours. Expect cross to be generally related to your direct testimony and rather pointed. It will be designed to reveal and exploit "soft spots" in your testimony. Expect leading questions that limit you to only short answers and, in many instances, seek only "yes" or "no" responses. Unlike questions asked during direct examination, which must not point to a response, cross by adverse counsel will attempt to "lead" you to an answer. Thus, a "leading question" is one in which the questioning attorney does the "testifying" and the fact sought to be established is contained in the question itself, requiring only a yes or no response. The plaintiff's attorney likely will present you with a series of factual statements and ask that you acknowledge the accuracy of each. Be careful to avoid readily accepting facts offered if you can legitimately reject them. Understand that cross-examination is designed to elicit your acknowledgment of facts that support the plaintiff's theory of the case.

Frequently, you will be confronted with statements in your records, interrogatory answers, and/or deposition testimony which might not be supported by facts referenced in other treatment records or which are inconsistent with facts offered by the plaintiff or recited by the plaintiff's expert. Of course, your attorney would have reviewed the potential areas of cross-examination with you during your pre-trial conferences so as to render you fully prepared. Having been fully prepped by your lawyer for cross-examination, you should rarely be surprised by any question that opposing counsel asks, and you certainly should be able to reasonably respond to cross-examination no matter how pointed. Always remember that, as with your deposition, you cannot be forced to answer a question at trial that you do not understand. You should simply state that the question is unclear and force adverse counsel to rephrase it.

Do not permit adverse counsel to box you in with a prefatory instruction that you respond "yes" or "no" to a given question. If a reasoned and intelligent answer precludes a simple "yes" or "no", it is unlikely that the trial judge will force you to provide the one-word response sought by the plaintiff's attorney.

Understand that the tenor of the cross will be dictated by the personality of the questioning lawyer and may not be predictable. Your attorney likely will be able to provide some insight as to what to expect from the plaintiff's counsel. Always anticipate a vigorous cross.

The manner in which you respond to cross-examination and the cross-examiner will be determined, in part, by your personality. Be yourself on the witness stand. Avoid being abrasive or smug. Don't be flip or glib and never be disrespectful or impatient. In a difficult spot, rely on who you are and what you know. Attorneys become attorneys by graduating from law school and passing a bar exam. That's it. With rare exception, lawyers, even those who specialize in malpractice, do not have the education, training, and experience possessed by you. They can't know what you know professionally and therefore can't go "toe to toe" with you. During tough cross, always fall back on what made you a capable and accomplished practitioner and use it.

Interpersonal Connection

People are people. This most elemental of axioms has real application to the courtroom. When testifying, it is your job to convince a group of strangers that you are worthy of belief. Achieving this goal requires that you connect with each member of the jury on an interpersonal level. Outside the courtroom, this task is far easier to achieve. In fact, the "connection" of which I speak occurs with some frequency. It occurs regularly in your personal life, and of course, it happens routinely in your professional life.

In a typical practice, the opportunity to connect with people exists every day and often. Each time you see a patient, you "connect". This human interaction is unforced, natural, and typically successful. If you were not capable of connecting with patients, new and old, you would not survive professionally. It really is no different in the courtroom. In fact, speak to the jury as you would to patients.

Whatever it is you do to establish and maintain relationships in your practice is what you must try to accomplish in court, albeit in an accelerated manner. That effort is defined by perhaps the most basic of human interactions – conversation. Think about what you do during a conversation to communicate your thoughts, to convince, to persuade. Those are the things you must do as a trial witness.

Unlike encounters in the real world, however, those that occur in court are the result of a deliberate design. The environment is created by circumstance to achieve the resolution of disputes. The participants, somewhat involuntarily, converge to air issues and to foster "debate" so as to permit previously unidentified individuals (jurors) to "arbitrate" disagreements and fashion remedies. It is in this environment that you must effectively "communicate". Unlike the more natural and familiar forums in which you daily encounter people, courtroom communication is only permitted in accordance with certain "rules". Persuasive "conversation", therefore, is more difficult. Within the confines of this environment, however, human connections nevertheless can be forged.

As already touched upon, perhaps the most effective method to achieve this is to address each juror as an individual. That is, rather than generally looking at the jury as a group, a deliberate effort must be made to develop a one-on-one "dialogue" with each juror. The goal is to make each jury member feel as though you are speaking directly to him or her. You can accomplish this by looking at each juror for a few moments while testifying as though he or she is being individually addressed. Given the typical length of direct testimony, this likely can be done repeatedly. The juror to whom you are speaking will feel engaged by your testimony and consequently will respond favorably to you as a witness.

Of course, the "yes" or "no" responses typically sought of a defendant by a plaintiff's lawyer during cross-examination will limit opportunities to speak to the jury at length. However, when they do occur, you should answer such questions posed by adverse counsel by talking directly to the jury.

A second and related aspect of the interpersonal encounter is eye contact. While speaking directly to each juror, it is imperative that you make eye contact. Again, direct testimony will consume a significant amount of time – certainly enough time for you to look into the eyes of each juror on multiple occasions. You must make a conscious effort in this regard. If you are able to make and sustain eye contact, the jurors will probably feel more comfortable with you. If you look away from the individual jurors, it is unlikely that you will make the necessary connection.

Be careful to avoid appearing as though your head is on a swivel. If your response to a given question posed during direct examination allows for but a brief response, there is no need to turn to the jury before answering. To do so and to do so frequently will make your testimony look contrived and can only serve to damage an otherwise credible presentation.

Testimony Content

The content of your responses to courtroom examination must be understandable, if not simple. Remember, the individuals you are addressing are not professional colleagues. Jurors will typically have no educational or practical foundation upon which to draw in an effort to comprehend what will customarily be rather complicated and complex concepts. At best, a juror's knowledge base usually will be limited to that gained from being a patient. Consequently, you must avoid defining difficult precepts with equally difficult explanations. The process requires "plain talking".

If you have taught or currently teach students or residents, you likely understand the "plain talking" notion, which is even more important in the context of trial testimony. Although you may consider the courtroom a classroom of sorts for the limited purpose of conveying your thoughts during a single "lecture", the challenge presented in the courtroom is somewhat different from that faced in the classroom.

Unlike those taught in the classroom, the "students" in the courtroom are not there by choice. By and large, they have no science background. They are not seeking a career in the very field you have selected as your own. In sum, they will not recognize or quickly absorb principles with which you routinely deal, and they are not provided with textbooks to review before, during, and after your testimony so as to promote concept reinforcement.

As a result, you must be able to convey your thoughts in a manner that optimizes the relatively brief time you have with the jury. Not only must the jurors understand what you are saying, but they must recall your testimony, or at least its most salient portions, when they deliberate, which in most trials will be days after you have testified. The more difficult the subject matter, the greater the challenge. It is not enough that you have the credentials and experience to know about the discrete treatment issues confronted during the course of care provided to the plaintiff. Without "talking down" to the jurors, you must also be able to explain those issues so that the jury understands and remembers. To that end, use universally recognizable terms. Where necessary, care must be taken to render otherwise complex topics to laypeople obvious and clear.

You must avoid responding to questions about complex concepts with vague, meandering, and/or unduly lengthy responses. Frankly, a jury's tolerance for testimony provided in this fashion is limited – in fact, very limited. If you are speaking directly to the jury, as you must and in the manner already described, you should be able to recognize when you have "lost" your audience. If the jurors' eyes appear to glaze over, the need to speak plainly becomes acute. In the alternative, if you notice the occasional approving head nods, you likely are effectively peppering your testimony with sufficient explanations and definitions. From the jury's perspective, simple testimony about complex matters is easier to understand and, ultimately, easier to recall.

Trial Aids

Bringing your testimony to life is key to persuading the jury. Given the proposition that, by definition, the content of expert testimony is beyond the knowledge of the average juror, enhancing that testimony indeed is a trial objective. Accomplishing that goal should be the focus of discussions with your lawyer during your trial prep meetings. In my opinion, trial aids are a means to that end and fall into two categories – verbal aids and physical aids.

Verbal aids are easily incorporated into trial testimony and at times are spontaneous. They typically take the form of analogies to life experiences that are easily identifiable by jurors. For example, if the subject matter is orthopedic surgery, you may liken bones, orthopedic hardware, and surgical instruments to wood, screws, and shop tools. Other examples are likening tendons to rubber bands and equating impeded blood flow in an obstructed vessel to water flow in a kinked garden hose. Some analogies are quite simple and some are less so. Some may be devised prior to trial and deliberately injected into your testimony at the appropriate time and some may come to mind during testimony. Either way, analogies drawn from common experience invariably assist in the jury's understanding of your testimony at the time offered and are easily recalled at the later and critical time of jury deliberations.

Make certain, however, that the verbal analogies you employ are those that can be offered in gender-mixed company. No matter how "cute" or "catchy", avoid those that can be interpreted as sexist or gender-biased.

As an example, in an effort to explain a medical condition, a witness spontaneously and surprisingly indicated that his description of the condition's severity could be easily understood by using a scale of "1 to 10", 10 being at the ultimate end of the range, "like Bo Derek". Those of you who understand the unexpected reference should also recognize that this sexist remark was ill-advised. I internally cringed at the moment, acutely sensitive to the comment. My hope, however, was that the gender-mixed jury would ignore and ultimately forget it.

The second type of trial aid is the physical one and can include anatomical models, drawings, photos, videos, enlarged documents, displays, PowerPoint slides, and computer-generated images. If there is one thing about which I am certain, it is the value of such demonstrative evidence. It serves to teach a juror in a manner that no spoken word alone can accomplish. Physical trial aids complement the verbal presentation and increase the jury's interest. They should be a planned focal point of your direct testimony, which will bring to life what might otherwise be perceived as boring, dry, uninteresting, or overwhelmingly complex. Once used during your direct testimony, these aids will be available to you for use during cross-examination as circumstances warrant. In fact, you may gain control of the cross by offering to use such exhibits during your responses.

In sum, demonstrative evidence makes you and your courtroom testimony better. Your attorney understands this very fact, and the use of such trial aids should be discussed with your counsel at the earliest pre-trial opportunity.

Expect that the courtroom will be equipped with a whiteboard or a large pad on an easel. When planned with your attorney, you should use it to create anatomical drawings to help explain your testimony. Of course, if you are incapable of effectively drawing parts of the anatomy (and many highly regarded and exceptionally competent practitioners simply cannot draw), don't attempt this in court before a jury. Instead, use a picture or poster that you already have in your office for patient education. Alternatively, locate a drawing in a textbook, journal article, or on a website. (I am particularly partial to the Frank Netter, M.D. published collection of anatomical illustrations, which are beautifully detailed, in color, and labeled.)

Three-dimensional models of the anatomy are also a favorite of mine and typically are fascinating to jurors. If you have a relevant anatomical model in your office, suggest using it to your attorney. Because of its three-dimensional value, a model is probably one of the most effective aids at trial.

Enlarging treatment records into poster-size exhibits or creating PowerPoint slides may also prove helpful. Testimony about matters recorded in a hospital or office chart may be lifeless and dull. However, placing an enlargement of those notes before the jury during your testimony will undoubtedly increase juror interest in their content and will render an otherwise mundane review of such entries more appealing.

With the existence of sophisticated computer-based software, attention should be paid to its use at trial. Laptops can be brought to court and connected to a large monitor, which can be found in most courtrooms. PowerPoint presentations and computer-generated images can be used during testimony in much the same way as more conventional drawings, pictures, and models are used. Once again, the goal is to render your testimony more understandable and interesting.

To the extent that the computer can assist in that process, it, too, should be considered a valuable trial aid.

Litigation support firms, medical illustrators, pharmaceutical companies, reproduction or graphic shops, photography studios, or photocopy stores can provide many if not all of the trial aids discussed and can be contacted by your counsel after you have discussed and selected the appropriate exhibits. Even AI can assist in the identification and creation of trial aids.

In addition, many manufacturers of medical devices, instruments, and prosthetic components produce and distribute videos of their products and their use, in various formats. Although typically created for review by practitioners or for patient education purposes, videos of this type, without the audio component, may serve a useful purpose. If your matter involves, for example, a certain prosthetic implant and the manufacturer of that item has produced an informational clip about that product, it may prove educational at trial and may serve to enhance your testimony. Assuming there are no evidential impediments to its use, this aid will likely be beneficial at trial.

Intangibles

In addition to the very palpable qualities already discussed, there exists one final value worthy of note. As is the case in everyday life, a positive human response to experiencing a new event or meeting a new person is dependent upon favorable stimulation of the senses. That is to say, often the "good feeling" enjoyed results not so much from an intellectual reaction but rather from a quasi-emotional one. If you feel "comfortable" speaking to a new acquaintance, that individual by word and/or by deed has triggered a positive response on many levels. As a trial witness, it is imperative that you secure a similar reaction in the jurors you seek to impress. Should you be successful in that effort, you may be more easily perceived by the jury as someone to be accepted and believed.

On direct examination, you must be certain of yourself and compelling in your testimony. Responding to cross-examination may present more of a challenge. However, if you are able to answer questions posed by adverse counsel with conviction but without an argumentative tone, it is likely that the jury, or certain of its members will find themselves recalling, and more important, supporting your testimony in the jury room during deliberations when it really counts. Indeed, transforming once uninformed jurors into disciples is the goal. Always remember that you must engage them during your testimony. Put the jurors at ease and then draw them in.

Of course, your lawyer will counsel you well in advance of the trial to make the most of your opportunity to favorably influence the jury from the witness stand. Both verbal and nonverbal communication will be key. However, it bears mentioning that you should always avoid direct contact with the jurors. You may innocently encounter jury members in the hall, elevator, or restroom or as you enter or exit the courthouse. Jurors may also be in a neighborhood restaurant or courthouse cafeteria. You must refrain from remarking verbally about your case or any aspect of the trial, no matter how innocuous, because a juror may overhear those remarks.

Summations

At the conclusion of testimony by all witnesses and the acceptance by the trial judge of documents offered in evidence by all counsel, the attorneys then present their Summations or Closings in the reverse sequence of Opening Statements. That is, the defense lawyers address the jury first. Thereafter, the plaintiff's attorney provides a Summation.

During Summations, counsel will review and remark about the evidence presented during the trial in a manner that best suits the client's position. Of course, your attorney will focus on the strengths of the case presented on your behalf. You should expect remarks about your credentials inclusive of your education and training and your experience in treating the very condition which is the subject of the trial. Compliance with the standard of care will be a focus of your counsel's Summation. Support for your attorney's closing argument will have been supplied by your liability expert's testimony and perhaps, to a certain degree, counsel's analysis of the short-comings of the plaintiff's expert's testimony exploited during your lawyer's cross-examination. If causation is an issue, as it typically is, expect commentary by your lawyer about the lack of evidence supporting the plaintiff's claim that your alleged negligent treatment caused injury to the plaintiff. Although money damages are always a trial issue, your lawyer likely will not spend much time addressing damages. Defense counsel rarely will talk about damages since doing so serves only to remind the jury of the damages component of the case, which your counsel would prefer be forgotten.

Instructions to the Jury

Upon the completion of Closings, the trial judge will Charge the jury. The Charge is the judge's reading of the applicable law, which the jurors are duty-bound to apply to the facts as established by the evidence. The Charge will identify the party who has the burden of proof as to each issue presented at the trial. In a basic malpractice case, the plaintiff must prove each element of a claim by a "preponderance" of the evidence. Of course, in a more complex matter, the defendant may bear the burden of proof as to certain issues

The term preponderance of the evidence is defined as the greater weight of the evidence. To establish malpractice, the scales of justice must be tipped ever so slightly in favor of the plaintiff who typically bears the burden of proof.

The trial judge also will mention that evidence offered to establish a claim must be credible or believable before it can be accepted by the jury. The court will identify the factors the jurors can consider in assessing the credibility of a witness. The judge also will explain that evidence presented in support or in defense of a claim can be direct or circumstantial. Of course, each type will be defined. As an example of direct evidence, the court might explain that a witness who sees snow falling at night could provide direct testimony that it snowed during the night. Circumstantial evidence of snow having fallen during the night might come from a witness who did not see snow falling before going to sleep but who upon awakening in the morning saw snow on the ground. This testimony would be an example of circumstantial evidence of snow having fallen overnight.

Depending on the number of issues presented, the Charge in a malpractice trial may consume 45–60 minutes. To some degree, the length of the Charge may be affected by how quickly or slowly the trial judge reads the Charge.

Routinely, each attorney will submit a proposed Jury Charge which recites the law that the lawyer would like the judge to read to the jury. The trial judge will consider the submissions of your counsel and that of the plaintiff's lawyer. Some of an attorney's proposals may be incorporated into the final Charge which the court will read to the jurors. In most jurisdictions, established "model" Charges exist, and the trial judge will utilize most of the model language since it recognizes and incorporates the existing law in that jurisdiction. A judge's Charge rarely will vary significantly from the state's model as to any legal concept, since to do so arguably will run afoul of established law. Perhaps there may be a multitude of ways to state a legal principle, and language changes proposed by counsel will be the subject of a "Charge Conference" with the judge. At times, the court may be persuaded to alter some of the language in the Charge. After some finessing, the final version is complete.

After the jury is "charged", the attorneys will be invited to sidebar by the Court where counsel will be permitted to identify any perceived errors in the Charge. Those errors may well be the result of inadvertence since a written version of the Charge typically would have been provided to counsel for review before being stated to the jury. Comments at sidebar by the attorneys after the Charge is delivered to the jurors likely will not be due to a substantive change in the Charge. Whatever issue is raised, it may be necessary for the Court to restate and clarify portions of the Charge.

Of course, you can ask your attorney for a copy of the Charge to review either before or after it's read to the jury. Seeing the law in writing may help crystallize the legal concepts that are applicable to your case. In some instances, a printed copy of the Charge is given to the jury. That may happen as a result of the particular trial judge's belief that the jury's understanding of the law is enhanced by seeing the law in print. In some jurisdictions, the practice of providing the jury with a written version of the Charge is dictated by local court rule.

A printed Verdict Sheet prepared by the Court will be provided to the jurors at or near the conclusion of the Charge. It will contain all the questions that the jury might consider and answer. Like the Charge, it will represent the collaborative effort of the trial judge and the lawyers. Routinely, trial counsel will submit a proposed Verdict Sheet for the judge to consider. It is not unusual for a jurisdiction to have standard questions to be asked of a jury in a malpractice case, which counsel can review in advance of the trial. Often, and prior to the conclusion of the trial, the lawyers nevertheless will draft proposed questions to be included in the Verdict Sheet, which will contain language preferred to that in the standard questions. At the Charge Conference, the trial judge will review the proposals and accept some or none of the offered language. The Verdict Sheet presented to the jury during the Court's Charge will be available to you to review. You will see the specific questions the jury will be asked to consider and potentially answer.

A Verdict Sheet in a very basic malpractice trial with issues of liability, causation, and damages may look like this sample:

Verdict Sheet

_____ v. _____
Docket No. xxxxx

1. Did the defendant deviate from the accepted standard of care in the treatment of the plaintiff?

Yes_____No_____

If your answer to question 1 is yes, proceed to question 2. If your answer to question 1 is no, cease your deliberations and return your verdict.

2. Was the defendant's deviation from the accepted standard of care a proximate cause of the plaintiff's injuries and damages?

Yes_____No_____

If your answer to question 2 is yes, proceed to question 3. If your answer to question 2 is no, cease your deliberations and return your verdict.

3. What amount of money would fairly and reasonably compensate the plaintiff for pain, suffering, disability, impairment, and loss of enjoyment of life?

Amount_____
Agree_____Disagree_____

Affirmative responses to both the first and second questions establish that you were negligent and that such negligence was a substantial cause of the injuries and damages alleged. The jury must then decide the amount of money to which the plaintiff is entitled. A negative answer to either the first or second question will result in a verdict in your favor. A positive response to the first question alone is insufficient to return a verdict for the plaintiff. In order for you to be found liable, the jury must determine that you acted negligently and that the negligent conduct was a proximate cause of the plaintiff's injuries and damages. A "proximate cause" is often defined as a cause that set other causes in motion and was a substantial factor in bringing about the injury. It is an event which naturally and probably led to, and might have been expected to produce the result.

Of course, a more complex case involving additional issues such as informed consent, aggravation of a preexisting medical condition, comparative negligence or mitigation of damages, or which includes a plaintiff's spouse or other defendants in addition to you, will lengthen the trial and complicate the trial proofs, resulting in an increase in the number of questions on the Verdict Sheet.

In states like New Jersey, eight jurors are usually selected at the beginning of a civil trial like a malpractice case. At the trial's conclusion, immediately after the Jury Charge as described above, two of the eight are randomly selected by computer as alternates, and the remaining six jurors will deliberate. Of course, if one or two jurors are excused during the trial due to illness or inability to serve for any other reason, the trial judge may only need to excuse one juror or perhaps no one before deliberations begin. During deliberations, if a juror unexpectedly is unable to participate, one of the alternates will take that juror's place.

In lengthy trials, a judge may be inclined to allow all eight jurors to deliberate. Usually, such thinking is prompted by the Court's belief that jurors who participate in a protracted trial should not be arbitrarily precluded from being part of deliberations. However, this is only permitted if your attorney and other counsel agree.

Jury Deliberations

After the Charge, the jury is instructed to retire to the jury room to begin deliberations. The jury members who have been selected as alternates will remain outside the jury room and will not be part of the deliberations. However, the Court will direct that each alternate remain in the courthouse or otherwise be physically available to serve as a replacement in the event a juror cannot continue to deliberate. Those circumstances include juror illness, a family emergency, or any urgent event that prevents a juror from participating in deliberations.

Alternates are chosen at random. Historically, the process of selecting alternates involved placing the names and numbers of the jurors on folded pieces of paper which were placed in a drum or basket that could be rotated. After a few spins, the court clerk would open the access door, reach inside and select the juror who would be identified as the alternate. If multiple alternates needed to be chosen, the process would be repeated. That process has given way to computer programs that randomly select alternate jurors.

Before the deliberating jurors leave the courtroom, the jury foreperson is selected. In many courts, the trial judge will identify the juror occupying the first seat in the jury box as the foreperson. In other courts, the foreperson will be selected randomly. Regardless of the system utilized, the foreperson has no greater power or authority than any other juror. Traditionally, the foreperson will be responsible for conducting an orderly discussion of the evidence and making sure each juror participates in the conversation. As will be more fully explained below, if the jury or an individual juror has a question that must be addressed by the trial judge, the foreperson will write the question on a piece of paper and give it to the court officer who will then provide it to the judge.

While the jury is deliberating, your attorney likely will ask that you remain in the courthouse until the jury has reached a verdict. Deliberations can take minutes or hours. In some instances, although rarely, deliberations in malpractice trials may consume a day or more. It is possible that your lawyer will allow you to leave the courthouse if, upon learning that the jury has reached a verdict, you are able to return within minutes.

Not infrequently, jurors have substantive questions about the testimony of a witness or an aspect of the Charge. Jurors are told as part of the court's instructions that if a question arises during deliberations, that question should be reduced to writing by the jury foreperson and given to the court officer who will provide it to the judge for review. When the jury has a question, all the attorneys will be advised. The judge then will inform counsel of the question and discuss with the attorneys the response the court intends to provide. Of course, the lawyers can offer suggested language to the judge. Everyone then is assembled in the courtroom, including the parties, so that the judge can provide the jury with an answer to the question. You should not be absent from the courtroom when the jurors appear to hear the trial judge's answer to their question. Your absence will be noted and at least subconsciously will not be appreciated. After hearing the court's response, the jury then will be directed to return to the jury room to resume deliberations.

A verdict in a malpractice trial need not be unanimous. With a six-member jury, a question on the Verdict Sheet is considered answered if at least five of the six jurors provide the same response. Importantly, the same five jurors need not agree as to each question. If all eight jurors deliberate as previously explained, a Verdict Sheet question is answered if at least seven jurors agree.

Once deliberations are concluded and a verdict is reached, the jury will advise the court by writing a note stating that it has a verdict and delivering that note to the court officer, who then provides the note to the court. Everyone is assembled in the courtroom, and upon the request of the trial judge, the foreperson announces aloud the answer to each required question. Upon the announcement of the verdict in open court, a judgment is entered in favor of the prevailing party, and the trial phase is formally concluded.

The trial also might end without verdict if the jury is hopelessly deadlocked. Although this happens rarely, it nevertheless can occur when the requisite number of jurors cannot agree on an answer to a necessary Verdict Sheet question. If the judge is satisfied that additional deliberations will not break the deadlock, the court will declare a mistrial. The jurors will be released from service and a new trial will be scheduled in the future with a new trial judge and a different jury.

Post Trial Motions

Motions seeking relief from the verdict may follow the end of the trial (almost always by the losing party), and an appeal may thereafter be filed. Otherwise, the end of the trial typically signals the end of the lawsuit.

If you should win the trial, the plaintiff's attorney may seek relief from the jury verdict by filing an application with the court. That application will be in the form of a written submission called a motion. It typically will identify a significant erroneous ruling on the evidence or the law by the trial judge that adversely impacted the trial's outcome and which under applicable law should require a new trial. Your counsel will submit a written response opposing the relief sought, seeking to preserve the jury verdict and consequent judgment.

The trial judge will hear oral argument by the lawyers and thereafter rule on the motion. Should the plaintiff prevail, a new trial will be scheduled many months later. A different trial judge will preside, and the jury selection process explained above will start again. Should your counsel prevail, the defense verdict and consequent judgment will remain undisturbed.

Of course, it may be your attorney who believes errors occurred during the trial resulting in a plaintiff's verdict. Defense counsel will submit a written motion requesting relief, with the plaintiff's lawyer submitting opposition. If your lawyer prevails, a new trial will be scheduled.

No matter who wins a new trial motion, the losing party has the right to file a written appeal with the appellate court seeking a review of the trial court's ruling. Adverse counsel will then submit written opposition. Oral argument will be conducted by the attorneys, and if the appealing party wins, the matter will be returned to the trial level for a new trial.

Lawsuit Experience

After enduring a trial, you will return to your practice with an appreciation for what the litigation process entails. Should you become a malpractice defendant again, you certainly will be well-prepared for the challenges of another lawsuit. You also might think differently about the medical and/or treatment issues that were raised by the case.

Of course, a favorable trial outcome will always make you feel better about the long and grueling process you were forced to endure. Though your emotional strength may have been tested from time to time, hearing the announcement of a defense verdict at the end of the trial will provide you with an unparalelled sense of relief and satisfaction.

Index

For Product Safety Concerns and Information please contact our EU
representative GPSR@taylorandfrancis.com
Taylor & Francis Verlag GmbH, Kaufingerstraße 24, 80331 München, Germany

www.ingramcontent.com/pod-product-compliance
Lightning Source LLC
Chambersburg PA
CBHW061331220326
41599CB00026B/5128

9 781032 604114